FAITH-MADE MILLIONAIRE

3 PILLARS FROM THE GOOD BOOK TO MASTER YOUR MINDSET, MORALS AND MONEY

MATT SAPAULA

FOREWORD BY PATRICK BET-DAVID

Published by *Self Publish -N- 30 Days*
WWW.SELFPUBLISHN30DAYS.COM

Printed in the United States of America

ISBN: 979-8-9866939-1-0

1. Faith 2.Financial Information 3. Educational 4. Business and Entrepreneurship

Matt Sapaula, *Faith-Made Millionaire*

My Father in Heaven, only by grace am I able to increase
my abilities. May you be glorified in all that I do.

Mom, those Scriptures you'd write on every letter or card
when I was in the Marines worked, after all.
Never doubt the power of a #PrayingMother.

Dad, your words were few, but your example always spoke volumes.
I pray this work honors you and the
last name you gave me.

Sheena, my BooBoo, you've multiplied everything I've given you.
You're my wifey, my battle buddy, my ride-or die,
my partner, and my best friend.

To my kids: Ruben, Maylani, Soledad, JoeJoe, and Jordan,
you are my legacy, and you all have the best parts of me. I am proud of you.
I believe in you and always want the best for your lives.

To my unborn decendants, I already see you in my mind.
I'll do my part to build our last name, and I look for-
ward to helping you take it further.
I love you!

TABLE OF CONTENTS

FOREWORD

BY PATRICK BET-DAVID

If I had to choose one word to describe Matt Sapaula, it would be:

COACHABLE.

Throughout all his success, Matt has been the most coachable person I've worked with. He doesn't just take cricism well; he demands to hear it.

He is eager to know his blind spots and weaknesses because he knows that's the only way to improve. He is hungry for knowledge and a sponge for information.

Matt also has strong values and principles. Not only do I trust him around my family and kids, but I've gone out of my way for my family to spend time with his so they can see the example he sets. Though, in many ways, he's the stereotypical "man's man"—a gym rat who loves sports and cigars—he's also an amazing listener and a compassionate husband, father, and friend.

In addition to being coachable, Matt is also a phenomenal coach. The way he listens shows that he cares. He's the guy who's constantly saying, "I appreciate you." What makes that statement unique is that you can actually *feel* that he means it.

If you have that same level of coachability—and it's a very high standard—you're going to get a lot out of this book. Let me be clear: I am not saying anyone can be like Matt Sapaula. He's a rare breed, and very few can match his work ethic.

What I am saying is that if you're as coachable as Matt, you have a very high chance of success. If you picked up this book, are open to learning, and are prepared to work, you're going to get a lot of answers. Day in and day out, Matt mentors and leads people without fancy degrees (or any degrees for that matter) and turns them into big earners who make their families proud.

His system works!

There are only a few leaders I know who can balance emotion and logic. Matt is one of them. This book does the same. It will inspire you because it will touch your heart while offering techniques to change your mindset. Matt will show you the importance of faith, staying physically fit, and managing your money, all of which are necessary to reach next levels of success.

Matt put everything he has learned about both success and failure over the past thirty years into this book. He served eight years on the front lines in Somalia, Africa, and the Persian Gulf as a decorated member of the United States Marine

Corps. Like many veterans, it was a rough transition to go back to civilian life. Just when he thought he had turned the corner by getting married and having a child, he hit another low. Adversity tested his faith. When he turned away from it, he made bad choices, and things got worse. When he turned back towards it, he became the powerful, humble, and wealthy man you see today.

It makes perfect sense that Matt and I met because of our faith. We were introduced by Pastor Dudley Rutherford, the Senior Pastor of Shepherd Church in Southern California. On the surface, Matt looked like a stud. He was charismatic, ripped, charming, and yet still humble and approachable. The mystery was figuring out why he struggled so much financially. On paper, he had all the traits to be a millionaire, but he was barely making ends meet.

I'm happy that he wrote this book because you may be in a similar place as Matt was when I met him. You know you have potential, and you just can't seem to figure out what's holding you back. I've been there, and Matt's been there. The lesson to take from Matt is that if you're coachable, have faith, and put in the work, success will follow. It's that simple. I didn't say easy. I said simple.

Because Matt is so coachable, he's a master at re-creating himself. Wherever you are in life, you can become whatever you want. Matt has done it multiple times. From the moment he came to the company, growth took off at rates we've never seen before. He'll be the last to tell you how quickly he had his first million-dollar year and how he'll do five times that soon. Yet, with every zero he adds to his net worth, he has stayed humble.

I'm proud to call him a friend and a partner.

Future looks bright! And even brighter if you are as coachable as Matt Sapaula.

Patrick Bet-David
Entrepreneur, founder and CEO
#1 *Wall Street Journal* bestselling author of *Your Next Five Moves*

Introduction

"For I know the plans I have for you," declares the Lord, "plans to prosper you and not to harm you, plans to give you hope and a future."

—**Jeremiah 29:11**

In one year, I got married, became a father, and filed for divorce and bankruptcy. My life crumbled before my eyes, and since I was the only one who created it, I was the only one who could change it. I had two-hundred and fifty dollars to my name, a number that wasn't much lower than my embarrassing credit score.

Ralph Waldo Emerson once said, "Your actions speak so loudly, I cannot hear what you are saying." In other words, I don't need to tell you how bad I screwed up. The proof was in where I stood.

I was no stranger to adversity. As a Marine who fought in the Persian Gulf and Somalia, Africa, I had been in the worst positions that the world can bring you. What made this hell unique was that I was the enemy who inflicted the damage on myself.

I admitted defeat by declaring bankruptcy—a reality that would stretch out unknowingly for the next seven years of my life. If you've also had to face your financial failures, you know how tough it is to live without credit. When you don't have money to pay your bills and go to bed at night worrying about how to feed your family, you can understand the emotional toll it takes. I wore this scarlet letter with shame and embarrassment.

Every time the phone rang, and when I swiped my debit card, I held my breath and felt a twinge in the pit of my stomach. Creditors attempted to contact me daily while landlords, realtors, and car dealerships smirked at me in the way they uniquely do.

It seemed like everything I touched fell apart. While serving in the Marines, I looked forward to overcoming challenges and dealing with the worst. I was trained to fight, practiced our techniques and gained confidence in being in the fraternity of the baddest war fighters the world has ever seen.

In my personal life, away from my brothers in uniform, I was not prepared to deal with the consequences of failing in relationships and my finances—which I knew was the result of my own poor choices.

Due to even more careless actions after declaring bankruptcy, life somehow got worse. I found myself in an area of no training to prepare for such brutal battles at home. The cycle of bad relationship choices continued, as I was already a single father of one, then to three children a couple years later. When I saw the harmful effects I left in my wake, I woke up to great pain in order to see my greater calling: becoming a good father, a leader, and providing for my children. This revelation became the catalyst for my growth. The love for my children runs deep into the core of who I am. I did my best but managing life while raising kids did not come with any military training, and on most days, I felt like a failure and depressed.

During my twenties, my actions failed to align with what I wanted because I had abandoned the morals, principles, and core values that I learned playing sports and in the Marine Corps. To my surprise, it appears that's not uncommon. A record-high 50% of Americans rate the overall state of moral values in the U.S. as "poor."[1]

If you're struggling now, it might be because you feel like you must make a choice between abiding by your morals and feeding your family. I've been there. I've also seen that getting back into alignment became what sparked my financial success.

I only share my story for you to see that, by applying five elements—faith, family, finances, fitness, and fun—you can achieve success beyond your wildest dreams. You don't have to be perfect to have faith work in your life. You don't have to come from a wealthy last name, have a pedigree upbringing, earn a college degree, or be the best student in school. You simply need to master your mindset, morals, and money—and I will you show you how.

---

[1]Megan Brenan and Nicole Willcoxon. Record-High 50% of Americans Rate U.S. Moral Values as 'Poor'.

Before I get back to telling you how I became "Money Smart Guy", repaired my financial life, rebuilt my family, married my soulmate, and became a first-generation millionaire, I want to share with you a little about my background.

No one has ever accused me of being the sharpest tool in the shed! I'm the son of immigrants from the Philippines, had a 2.2 GPA in high school, started at the bottom rank in the Marines and still today, have no college degree. Your background doesn't define you; your actions do! Over the years, I mastered how to apply faith to my mindset, morals, and money. Faith can be interwoven into every part of our lives; all we must do is learn how to apply it.

You have this book in your hands because I know you can do it as well. I say that because, as a leader in business, I have mentored directly and indirectly hundreds of people who were nearly broke and watched them become six and seven-figure earners. Yes, I have a formula that takes people from any walk of life—some who speak English as a second language and many who barely graduated high school—and turn them into cash-flow millionaires if they're willing to do the work.

I've seen people with the least that end up doing the most because they kept their faith. When it came time to quit, when they hit a low point or doubted themselves, they doubled down on their faith and came out winning. In their worst moments, they channeled their faith and ended up changing the meaning of their last name to one that will be respected and admired in their bloodline forever.

I'm telling you this because the process works for anyone. I'm giving you a formula that can change your life in ways you have never imagined.

My mother immigrated from the Philippines to the United States where she knew no one, to become a nurse with just one hundred dollars to her name. My father, a charismatic tour guide in Manila, Philippines, befriended a client. The client owned an airline and asked my father if he wanted to come to the states to go to college. My father agreed and moved to America, where he eventually met my mother.

I grew up around a church but never really "in it." As the years wore on, I chose my own path and lustful desires. Translation: I thought I had all the answers and didn't need church, God, or faith. Unfortunately, I had hardened my heart because of insecurities, misplaced pride, and the seduction of external pleasures. It didn't take long to show up in how I lived my life.

I had a middle-income upbringing, but my family rarely discussed money during dinner or other conversations. I grew up taking the bus and train everywhere. I bought my first car after returning from my first deployment only to have someone break into it after I deployed again. So, I naively connected money to scarcity, pain and trying to endure hard times instead of building and sustaining wealth. Life pulled me in every direction without clarity, mental stability, or financial security until I established the right mindset, attitude, and morals.

Finally, after two decades in the financial industry, I learned how to build wealth, control my income, and continue multiplying it because of faith-based principles. In this book, I'm going to show you how to do it as well.

Before we continue, I want to manage expectations. This book is *not* intended to sell you on my belief systems, force any religion upon you, or recruit you into anything. Whatever your faith is, I respect it. What I'm telling you is that digging into your own faith and values—whatever they may be—will do wonders for your business, relationships, personal finances and life.

In this book, I will share what I have learned throughout many years (and many mistakes) regarding mindset, morals, and money and how they all interlock. Over the last two decades, I have studied and implemented principles from some of the greatest entrepreneurs who have lived. I've read books like *Rich Dad, Poor Dad* by Robert Kiyosaki, *The Power of Positive Thinking* by Norman Vincent Peale, and *Secrets of the Millionaire Mind* by T. Harv Eker, to name a few. Even one of my worst moments, which came soon after my wife and I got married, was captured in the book *Your Next Five Moves*, the bestseller written by my friend and mentor Patrick Bet-David.

I discovered that many of the written lessons from these books originate from the Bible. I've met countless successful entrepreneurs, multi-millionaires and billionaires from all over the world who have *never* gone to church on Sundays. Yet, they all use faith-based values and principles to get them to where they are without ever knowing it comes from a Higher Power.

Throughout each chapter, I will incorporate several parables that Jesus taught as well as other Scriptures that touch on the subject of faith. The same stories that impacted the apostles back then can still speak to us now and teach us valuable lessons for both business and life.

We can sum up what you're going to learn in three pillars:

1. Faith and family
2. Finance
3. Fitness and fun

You may see them as individual categories, but if you neglect or abandon one, they all suffer. Here's a brief overview of each:

Faith: All of us have faith in something, even those that do not believe in God or the Big Man Upstairs. We all have the intrinsic need to believe in something, to have a purpose greater than ourselves. For me, my faith is Christianity and having salvation through Jesus.

Family: It is imperative to keep family first. I have been given the tall order to provide, teach, love, support, and equip my family with a framework of vision and values. My family teaches each other, serves one another, and shares life's joys and challenges.

Finances: Money is not the most important thing; however, everything you want to do or desire to improve will have a road leading back to money. Providing for my family is one of my most important priorities. I need resources to maintain and improve the quality of life for those I love and care about.

Fitness: Health is your first wealth. The benefits of taking care of yourself are priceless and endless. Therefore, it is crucial to improve your daily activities. I want to show you everything I know to increase your chances of living a long, abundant life filled with contribution, helping yourself and others make a difference.

Fun: If you are not having fun with something, then why do it? Take time for reflection, education, exercise, recreation, and good old-fashioned fun. I love a good cigar and whiskey coupled with great conversation, pulling pranks or feeling the excitement of coppin' the newest drop of Air Jordans. We all must make time for ourselves to enjoy life the fruits of our labor.

In each section, I will share the principles which have transformed how I view *and* live out the specific area. I encourage you to take the time to assess these five areas of your life.

If you picked up this book with the expectation of making seven figures by the time you finish reading it, just know that every good thing comes with action and consistent effort over an extended period of time. There's a reason why the wealth of 80,000 crypto millionaires and innumerable NFT owners have evaporated in the first six months of 2022. King Solomon, the wisest and richest king who ever lived, said, "Wealth from get-rich-quick schemes quickly disappears; wealth from hard work grows over time" (Proverbs 13:11). Plus, I hope you don't expect me to walk on water as I am simply a man doing his best to grow and do the most with what he has.

I didn't get rich quick, nor do I know anyone who was able to sustain wealth without putting in the work and using the principles I outlined in this book. If you are committed to putting in the work, being consistent, willing to recreate yourself, and mastering all five elements, I *know* you can attain a seven-figure income and net worth. Becoming a millionaire is becoming more frequent these days and with inflation eating away at our money, becoming a millionaire will not be a luxury but a must.

If I had access to the information that I share in this book in my twenties, I would've known the ramifications stemming from the ripple effect of wrong decisions in all areas—relationships, entrepreneurship, and furthering my financial foundation. No one taught me what bankruptcy was until it was discharged. No one around me knew how a mutual fund worked or why life insurance outside the military, or your job, was important. As a result, I had no interest in pursuing deeper financial literacy until my back was against the wall. I had no choice but to start righting my wrongs the hard way. Since then, I've made it my mission to share my mistakes so others can avoid them.

While others call themselves a "self-made" or "team-made millionaire," I call myself a "*faith*-made millionaire." Faith aided me in mastering the aforementioned areas of my life to reach my level of success today. Using faith-based, biblical principles that have transcended human history and therefore became my foundational blueprint of choice.

I'll say to you what I say to everyone I lead. If you show you want something in life, I will do my part to help you. However, you have to take a faith step forward, listen and hopefully apply what I share with you. Nothing will make me happier than hearing your success stories of how you changed the course of your family legacy.

God will give you an opportunity. It's up to you to get up and do something about it. Your age, gender, race, education, upbringing, current financial status, or anything else cannot hinder you from generational wealth and a successful life. You can start now! So let's do this.

PILLAR I

FAITH & FAMILY

"The greatest legacy one can pass on to one's children, and grandchildren is not money or other material things accumulated in one's life, but rather a legacy of character and faith."

— **Billy Graham**

1

Misconceptions of Faith

"Faith is to believe what you do not see. The reward of faith is to see what you believe."

— **Saint Augustine**

Every human being lives by faith. Even someone who doesn't believe in a God or a Higher Power believes in science. They put their trust in hypotheses advanced by non-religious scientists with regard to the origin of the universe and questions of ultimate meaning. Since these are things they cannot scientifically verify, they essentially learned from others they consider authoritative.

Hebrews, chapter eleven in the Bible has often been called "The Faith Chapter." It describes many of God's greatest servants and how their faith enabled them to perform great acts and miracles and endure severe trials. This chapter says, "Now *faith is* the *substance* of things hoped for, the *evidence of things not* seen" (Hebrews 11:1, emphasis added).

Faith involves evidence of things *not* seen, but how can evidence be related to something unseen since evidence usually involves tangible things? In a courtroom, evidence involves facts—and anything that isn't seen—is hearsay.

Faith involves assurance of things we hope for, but if something is *hoped* for, that means it hasn't been received yet. Therefore, where faith is involved, there is an assurance that it will be received! Authentic faith, in any of God's promises, is *actually* the evidence.

If God promises to do something, it is impossible for Him to lie (Hebrews 6:18). Faith, by its very nature, produces action. We are wired to feel and act in accordance with what we believe to be true. We cannot help it. Faith is knowing what needs to be done without feeling prepared to make a decision. You don't have the skills or know what the end result will be, but you know there's a Higher Power that is seeing things through.

For years, I misunderstood faith. I used my faith in God as armor or insurance policy because I was either scared or looking for another layer of protection like I did in the military. I wanted eternal security just in case something happened to me.

I convinced myself that I was pleasing God, while in fact, God wanted me to use faith in my everyday life, not when I was about to cross into eternity.

If beliefs about God and faith abound, then misguided misconceptions about faith in Him also exist. I won't attempt to dispel every misconception about faith because that would take too long. I will share, however, some of the most common false beliefs we can hold regarding faith.

Misconception: God isn't concerned about money.
Truth: God cares about you and your money.

Some people believe God cares more about their heart and spirit versus what they do with their money. He actually cares about both. Half of Jesus' parables instruct people on how to handle earthly treasures. One out of ten verses in the four gospels deals with money and stewardship. Are you convinced yet? God taught more about stewardship than about Heaven and Hell combined!

Why in the world would God spend so much time on this topic if it wasn't necessary? Money is a training ground for God to develop (and for us to discover) our trustworthiness. "If therefore you have not been faithful in the use of unrighteous mammon, who will entrust the true riches to you?" (Luke 16:11).

Billy Graham once said, "You tell me what you think about money, and I will tell you what you think about God." If you look at your checkbook or financial records, you will see where your heart is. Money reveals the condition of our hearts, and how we deal with it shows how much we give over to our Lord versus how much we hold back.

Misconception: God will provide.
Truth: God entrusts us to be good stewards of what He gives us.

Since the beginning of time, God has placed renewable resources upon the earth sufficient to feed, clothe, and house all the people and animals who have ever lived upon the earth. However, it requires us to be in a partnership with Him.

God provides resources, opportunities, people, and wisdom. For example, life insurance isn't a religion nor our Creator, but it is a tool our Creator gives us to protect and provide for our family. It creates an instant financial estate to begin creating generational wealth.

Many people use religion and ignorance of God's Word to justify staying broke, yet they purchase a home and car with insurance. People will insure where they live and what they drive before leaving an inheritance for their family (Proverbs 13:22). People can be so heavenly-minded that they are no earthly good. If we aren't careful, we can let religion get in the way of being resourceful and responsible.

Misconception: Faith is for weak people.
Truth: My strength is finite—no matter how much weight I bench press or how many miles I run.

Strength comes when I own up to my weakness. It is tough to look in that mirror and see things you hate. How would I know I would go to Heaven if I never returned home? I refused to leave any box unchecked or stone unturned.

In my weakness, I depend on God. His strength flows through me and gives me the courage to improve. "*He does not faint or grow weary*; his understanding is unsearchable" (Isaiah 40:28, emphasis added). God's strength will never, ever give out.

Misconception: Good is 'good' enough.
Truth: We are saved by grace (that is, a gift) through the medium of faith and not by our own merit.

Years ago, I believed being a "good person" or doing a few nice things here was good enough to get me in good standings with the Big Man Upstairs. As long as I checked off a few good deeds, my heavenly insurance policy for life after death remained effective and enforced.

Life quickly caught up to me, and I sought out external pleasures and pushed God aside so I could live the life I desired. I would only seek Him if I needed to file a claim in the event of an emergency, but I abandoned Him when I believed things were going well.

Because we can never be good enough to get into Heaven, Christ's sacrificial life, death, and resurrection is the way to Heaven and a prosperous life. I could only live up to portraying I was good for so long until I started making some bad decisions, one right after the other. As we all know—decisions—good or bad, bear consequences. The reason we must make the right decisions is for our benefit. Unfortunately, I disobeyed God and entered into several wrong relationships. As a result, my choices harmed me and countless others.

My irresponsibility immensely impacted my three older children. They endured pain and confusion as they split their time between two homes. So much of my time with my kids was spent unwinding what they were taught when they returned to my house. It's tough when the other party does not share the same values and principles.

Misconception: Trusting God solves all your problems.
TRUTH: Faith helps you embrace the hardships of humanity.

When you know you are serving a greater calling, it helps you fight through your difficulties. Through setbacks, you are being refined and defined for your destiny. As a result, you view problems as opportunities to improve and seek solutions instead of quitting.

God isn't a magic genie who will grant wishes. Instead, He gives principles and encouragement through His Word to guide us in our lives. His promises strengthen us and give us the solution along the journey.

Misconception: Grace lets me do what I want.
TRUTH: God's grace saves us through faith in Christ. Good works will *result* from a true saving faith.

Living life on our own terms seems fun at first, doesn't it? Oh, come on—you can admit it! No judgment here. Our mind, logic, and experience tell us that we need to change, but, nevertheless, we do what we want to until we are completely depleted. Therefore, anyone who tells us we can escape the penalty for our actions and still enjoy life arouses a considerable degree of interest. It did me, anyway.

Romans 6:1 says, "What shall we say, then? Shall we go on sinning so that grace may increase? By no means! We died to sin; how can we live in it any longer?"

We must clearly understand that Scripture talks about a lifestyle of sin, not just a single act or two of failure. The writer here is talking about Christians who go on living an absolutely unchanged lifestyle while still claiming to have committed their lives to Christ. I did this for a while.

When I was seventeen, I joined the Marine Corps. There I had an unforgettable encounter that began the journey of my faith.

OPERATION RESTORE HOPE

"If you don't come back tonight, do you know where you will end up?"

The question caught me entirely off guard. Part of me wanted to brush it off, but I couldn't.

I had been in the Marines a little over a year, and I was on my first deployment. My team and I were preparing for a mission at 0300 to assault the beaches of Mogadishu. I had walked to the hangar bay area to properly position my armor where I would be sitting. While fixing the helicopter armor, I had to make sure I had the correct body armor because the last thing

I wanted to do was take a bullet up the *arse*—for lack of a better term.

A Navy sailor walked up to me as I was finishing up. If you know anything about the relationship between Marines and the Navy, you already know this was not common. Even though we were on their ship, Marines were in charge. The Navy ship was our Uber, and we weren't closely connected to anyone other than our own.

This complete stranger approached me with boldness, met my gaze, and asked, "Excuse me, Marine. If you don't come back tonight, do you know where you would end up?"

I glanced over my shoulders to make sure he was talking to me. "Are you talking about me dying tonight and going to heaven?"

"That's exactly what I'm talking about," he said.

In the most non-confident tone, I shrugged and answered, "Yeah, I'd go to Heaven."

"Brother, do you want to be certain you'd go to heaven if you died tonight?"

I paused, mulling and stuttering over my answer. I thought, *you know what, I don't care if he's in a Navy uniform; he's speaking truth to me.*

"Please do," I said with a nod. "Tell me what I need to do."

"If you want to make sure that happens, please meet my shipmate and me in the ship's library downstairs in two hours."

"I'll do that if you promise me one thing," I said, silently praying he'd oblige my request.

"What is the promise?"

"Don't tell any other Marines I'm meeting you because I don't want them to know."

He smiled and nodded in agreement. In the back of my mind, I questioned what I was doing and why I was doing it, but I felt compelled to go.

The sun began to set so I headed to meet the sailor. I cautiously made my way to the ship's library, ensuring no one saw me. As I walked into the library, I skimmed the room, trying to spot the sailor quickly. To my surprise, I was welcomed by my entire platoon of Marines seated before the Navy sailors. It turned out I wasn't the only Marine he convinced to meet with him.

"Listen, you're about to head to the enemy's camp into battle," one seaman said. "You're not alone. God is with you now, but I want to make sure you have the assurance of going to Heaven."

What started as a pep talk turned into a call to salvation. Enamored by the message, I held on to every word. By the meeting's end, some Marines near me were wiping tears from their eyes.

"If you want to receive Jesus as your Lord and Savior," the seaman said. "Bow your heads and say this prayer."

I prayed as I had never prayed before. I did not want my life to end that night. After I lifted my head, a sense of calm washed over me. It's a feeling that is still hard to explain with words. I knew then I would go to Heaven if I would've died that night.

After the men closed the meeting in prayer, they began singing a cappella. The melodious sounds echoed through the library like they were singing on stage with a sound system. Worship broke out, a wave of emotions filled the room, and tears of strength and courage welled in our eyes. Praising God, we lifted our hands, and tears rolled down our cheeks.

That sailor made it his mission to share about Jesus if we didn't know Him. He made sure that we had that opportunity. None of the men who attended that meeting would be atheists in a foxhole.[2]

I never got to properly thank Brother White and Brother Johnson on the USS Tripoli in 1993. So if either of these men is somehow reading this book, I hope you find a way to reach out to me because I want to thank you for sharing the truth with me and my platoon.

God's grace saves us through faith in Christ. Good works will *result* from a true saving faith. Thus good works are *evidence* of faith. This is very different from saying that we are saved by being a good person because the Bible teaches that God's grace saves us through faith.

---

[2]The phrase is often attributed to war correspondent Ernie Pyle as an aphorism used to argue that people will believe in, or hope for, a higher power in times of fear or stress, such as during war ("in foxholes"). In our case, it was salvation through Jesus Christ.

While God's grace was given to me, I still spent the next decade of my life on the fence about what living out faith looked like. Without guidance or a spiritual mentor, I held on to salvation while still doing what I wanted to do. It wasn't until I saw my life flash before my eyes that I finally chose my faith over my desires.

As a single dad of three, I spent a ridiculous amount of money on things I thought would make me happy from age twenty to thirty. I showered my income on parties, clubs, bottle service, and unhealthy relationships. So on my thirtieth birthday, I wanted to get out and have a good time. I dropped my children off with my parents and headed to celebrate.

I had worked in insurance for a few years and finally reached a yearly salary of a couple hundred thousand dollars. So why go small? I shut down a bar in downtown Chicago on Saturday night.

People I hadn't heard from in years came out of the woodworks to celebrate. Even though they failed to support me initially, my pride and ego welcomed them. I bought them drinks all night—the more, the merrier, right? I was the man!

Before I knew it, the sun began to rise. I left the club and made it to my car. After strapping on my seatbelt, I put the key into the ignition and headed to the house to sleep off the liquor. Within minutes of driving, I could barely keep my eyes open.

I started drifting to sleep behind the wheel. At the same time, I found myself driving on the opposite side of the road with a car headed directly toward me. My heart was racing profusely. The other driver veered left, and I veered right, only seconds of missing each other. Thankfully, I got control of the car because I was going only thirty-five miles per hour.

Seeing that I was five feet away from hitting the bus stop on the opposite side of the road, I whipped to the right to get back in the correct lane.

Thank God no one else was on the road. As soon as I got in the right lane, I pulled over in one of the empty parking spots and set the gear in park. Then, gripping the steering wheel with both hands, I yelled, "What the hell are you doing, man? Why are you doing this?"

I peered in the rearview mirror and saw the other car's tail-lights in the distance. My life had flashed before my eyes. Here I was—a single dad with three kids who depended on me. My selfishness would have resulted in abandoning my kids. I could have killed myself—or worse, I could have killed some-one's loved one who was innocent due to my lack of personal judgment.

I liken my experience to Apostle Paul's encounter on Damascus Road (Acts 22:6-11). God had gained my attention and showed me that doing things my way had blinded me from seeing what He was doing in my life, particularly in that last decade of my life.

If my life was so much better without God, I wouldn't have found myself on the side of the road contemplating every life choice I had made after almost killing myself.

2

Act on Faith

"In the same way, faith by itself,
if it is not accompanied by action, is dead."

—James 2:17

A few hours after I almost wrecked my car, I pulled into a church parking lot. I still had the malodorous stench of alcohol from the night before. However, I decided to stay in the city and attend church since my friend had invited me for a while.

When I entered the foyer, a lady smiled at me and said, "Oh, you're here."

What are you talking about? I thought. *I don't even know you.*

It was almost like she was expecting me, but I never found out who she was. She wasn't a mutual acquaintance, and I don't recall seeing her after that.

As soon as she opened the door to the sanctuary, a rushing wind hit me on my face. Immediately, I sobered up. It was like I had never drank a drop of liquor.

The pastor began preaching a message that spoke straight to my heart. He talked about carrying our own burdens and how we end up trying to do things our way, so we refuse to let God help us.

During the altar call, the pastor said, "If you feel like the world is on your shoulders, let Jesus carry the weight. Let Him help you with what you are going through."

I thought *I'd lived my life my way for thirty years, and I didn't have the results I wanted. So, let me try it your way, God.*

That morning at church, I set aside my desires in order to fully trust God. I wanted to understand what life would be like to have and *use* faith, especially when I could not tangibly hold, store, or see through to the other side.

I stood up and made my way to the altar. I prayed with the pastor and let go of the weight I had been carrying. It was like a heavy burden lifted off my shoulders, and I believed I was on my way to becoming a better man.

ALL-IN

During this time, my life was confronted by this truth: Faith is a series of intentional actions. So, I started attending church regularly, reading my Bible, and searching for answers.

I finally stopped treating my faith as another piece of armor that I can take on and off at my convenience without it being a lifestyle. Just like Paul wrote two-thirds of the New Testament to teach others after his Damascus experience, I'm writing this book to show you how faith in God changes everything.

Life is so much bigger than just me. I want as many people as possible to be free from everything God has freed me from—limited beliefs, debt, PTSD, anger, depression, mediocrity, and the list goes on.

I dove all in and committed to trusting that things would work out—no matter how the current situation looked. For those who believe God is a figment of one's imagination, I'm not here to change or question your beliefs. However, if you want different results than what you are experiencing right now, it may require you to believe something different.

Knowing the definition of faith is one thing. Having faith and putting your faith to work? That's something else altogether. I'm here to tell you—if you say you have faith but fail to apply any principles, you are lying to yourself. Harsh? Maybe. True? Definitely. I could write an entire book on this subject, but I'll keep it in one chapter for now.

I wanted more than just a feel-good message and eternal life. I needed instructions on *how* to live my life. Change didn't happen immediately, but I was at a place in my life where I refused to continue down the path I was on. I knew I needed to take the necessary steps to show my dedication. Since I've done this, I've been committed to sharing the strategies I've used.

Every time faith is demonstrated in the Bible, it involves a specific promise along with action. A promise can contain healing, answers to prayer, receiving blessings (James 1:4-8), guidance in a difficult decision, or a business opportunity. Exponential progression follows when you use faith. Our decisions, desires, and what we do are connected to our thoughts and understanding, along with what we deem as truth.

For example, we have to *decide*—or commit to things that serve and help us grow. If we don't follow through with the decision to use faith daily—our desires (or thoughts) will have us doing (actions) the same things we've always done. Therefore, our lives stay the same.

Because much of our spiritual life is beyond intellectual comprehension, many people don't invest time or effort in deepening their faith and learning principles to benefit their lives. Therefore, they bypass what their lives can be because God's promises are only given to those who use the Word—and you can't use the Word if you don't know it. Faith creates actual, tangible results when you implement it how it is designed. It took my entire thirties to obtain this revelation to restore the mistakes I made in my twenties. I should have experienced the life I'm currently living a decade ago, but because I delayed doing things God's way, I delayed the calling He had for me.

I'm grateful my life was spared to receive "all the things" because I finally decided to seek the kingdom of God and all His righteousness first (Matthew 6:33)—keyword *first.*

Praying and asking for God's help doesn't mean you become lazy and do nothing. On the contrary, if you say, "Well, I'm still waiting on God. I'm still waiting for ... (fill in the blank). I've got to pray about it and wait on the Lord to answer," religion has you indecisive and complacent.

Pray like it's up to God and work like it's up to you. You cannot work yourself into Heaven, but you can work to have a successful life.

Many of us in the church always hear, "Faith without works is dead," but we forget the second verse. Part b of James 2:18 says, "Show me your faith without deeds, and I will show you my faith by my deeds."

James points out that what we do results from what we believe. Simply claiming to have faith in Christ is meaningless; saving faith is a faith that results in action. James describes any work, from works of kindness to starting a business. Work is meant to be continual. Our works reveal where our faith is. Jesus told us that a "tree is known by its fruit" (Matthew 12:33).

God's help shows up after we have prayed and put feet to our faith. I wasn't sure what would happen, but I always had comfort in knowing that tomorrow would be better. So, I got up to work every day, and God would strategically align things up. I would make the right phone calls and be introduced to the right people.

The first thing I did was align my values with God's Word. Then I came to a place in my life when I had to stop only *believing* and start *doing.*

VALUES

Values are the compass in life that tell us what is right and wrong. They set our standard for what we choose to do. Our personal values and beliefs have a powerful effect on our lives. We often form our beliefs about our world and ourselves when we are young.

I'm reminded of Gandhi's words, "Your beliefs become your thoughts. Your thoughts become your words. Your words become your actions. Your actions become your habits. Your habits become your values. Your values become your destiny."

If you keep getting stuck in the same place and don't understand why—I have great news: your values are not inscribed into your DNA. They are learned and have developed and grown in you since your birth. They bubbled to where they are today because of your environment, experiences, events, and decisions in your life. This means you are able to change them!

It is essential to know your core values and live by them. If you want to discover what your values truly are, ask yourself these questions:

- What is most important to you in life?
- What makes things valuable for you?
- Where do you spend the best of your time and energy?
- What are your deep concerns?
- What most excites you in life?
- What personal values resonate most with you to live an extraordinary life?

Below are some of the values I established in my life. They now have become The Sapaula Family Values which I review with my kids regularly. These ideals serve as a guide for their decisions as they get older.

Wisdom: Seek more than just knowledge.

Knowledge X Experience = Wisdom

Initiative: Don't wait for anyone or anything to do something for you. Go after it.

Gratitude: Appreciate and love what you have and who is in your life. Never focus on what you don't have.

Integrity: Always do the right thing, especially when no one is watching.

Dream: Life is not just existing; it is about what you can create to benefit yourself and others.

Beliefs—good or bad—unconsciously guide our lives. We have things we've learned from childhood and observing others—family, friends, people, and the culture around us. We take in the world around us and absorb information. As we form beliefs about life and ourselves, we are unaware of what they are and the power they have over us. As we get older and start to find our way in the world, we form values of what is important to us and how we want to live. When I started shifting my beliefs and values, I began understanding what it meant to renew my mind.

My bookshelf housed numerous New York bestsellers on mindset and thinking positively, but the Good Book is what helped me continuously renew my mind.

RENEW YOUR MIND

We are responsible for the pursuit of our mind's renewal. How do we accomplish this? How do we cultivate a renewed mind with thoughts, deliberations, and ideas that help us achieve a better understanding and positive outlook? Well, I'm glad you asked. Here are three steps that have transformed my mind:

2. Saturate Your Mind

Keep your mind on your faith. Peter calls Christians to "desire the pure milk of the word, so that you may grow up into your salvation" (1 Peter 2:2). This is an ongoing process throughout our lives. Yet, we must do more than read the Bible only; we must meditate on it.

In addition to reading and meditating, you can receive God's Word by sitting under sound preaching, listening to audio Bible readings, and, of course, memorizing different verses. But, whatever the means, the first key is to fill your mind.

2. Secure Your Mind

If filling your mind refers to what you take in, securing your mind refers to what you keep out. It can be a challenge to set barriers—especially in the beginning. We live in an age of visual saturation, ever-present social media, and pursuing temptation.

Temptation is a matter of the heart and the mind. The information we let in, the thoughts we entertain, and the ideas we foster can do much good or evil. Our mind is a powerful tool, for better or worse. What we think about, in many ways, determines the direction of our spiritual lives.

That is why the Apostle Paul exhorts us accordingly, "Finally, brothers and sisters, whatever is true, whatever is honorable, whatever is just, whatever is pure, whatever is lovely, whatever is commendable—if there is any moral excellence and if there is anything praiseworthy—dwell on these things" (Philippians 4:8).

3. Structure Your Mind

Not only are we to fill our minds and secure them, but we are to also structure them as well. Therefore, we must intentionally cultivate a paradigm through which we view and interpret the world.

We do this by applying the truth to our perspective. The truth gives us a solid foundation to engage in life. I realized it's possible to believe God exists yet not live a life that reflects it.

Mark 2:18-22 tells the parable of the old wineskins. The Scripture shares men do not put new wine in old wineskins because the skins would burst, and the wine would spill. This is a universal principle. Before truth can come into the mind, errors must be removed. If you pour wine into the old wineskins—it is hard and brittle. And if you pour too much, it could explode.

When you're trying to adopt a new way of approaching finances, or anything for that matter, you must view it with a renewed mind. If you want to learn about insurance, you may have to let go of most of what you've been taught.

If you want to expand your financial literacy capacity, yet your beliefs are built on old mindsets and stereotypes, you won't grow—no matter how much someone pours into you. Therefore, you must come into every circumstance with a new wineskin mindset and attitude for your mind to be shaped and molded.

Constantly refresh how you look at things. Networking and attending conferences and other events benefit you because it exposes you to new perspectives and information. Even if you have some resistance at first, you get to see them from a different position.

Furthermore, in Romans 12:2, Paul writes, "Do not conform any longer to the pattern of this world, but be transformed by the renewing of your mind." Transform your mind and stick to the values that serve your God-given dreams so that you may be a blessing wherever you go. Many times, it will mean swimming against the world's current, but the harvest you will reap will be worth it.

Renewing the mind will never work if someone constantly makes excuses. You cannot have miracles in your life regularly if your mind is a mess and you're fixated on making everyone responsible for where you currently are in your life. Your faith will get weaker the more you try to combat it with lies that you aren't capable of overcoming certain situations.

If my life was so much better without God, why did I find myself on the side of the road contemplating every life choice I had made? God spared my life for a reason, and since then, I have been determined to find out why.

ELIMINATE EXCUSES

Benjamin Franklin said, "The man who is good for excuses is good for little else." Unfortunately, many people like to make excuses rather than make things happen. This lifestyle paralyzes their progress and halts their blessings!

For example, some people still make excuses about what someone can't do today based on certain laws regarding race and gender in the 1950s—1980s. Now, I know I'm touching on a very sensitive subject here. In the past, my upbringing, race, family, last name, finances, and credit score has prevented me from achieving certain things. (Don't forget my credit score was not just low—it was in the 450 range, which was lower than low.) However, I rose above and refused to let my race, surname, or upbringing dictate how much money would be in my bank account.

Now that I own a business, I don't care about any race or the color of people's skin. There's only one race I care about—the human race. There's only one color that I pay attention to—and that is the color green. (That's money for those of you who missed that.)

While race can be an excuse for some people in order to succeed, disabilities can be an excuse for others. For example, a guy on my team has a hearing and learning impairment, yet he still invites guests to our meetings and fully embraces every opportunity to help others.

His sister translates for him so we can understand what he wants to tell us. This young man could easily use his disability to sit at home and do nothing. But instead, he comes up to our office pumped and excited to be a part of the team. His positive spirit and faith uplifts others.

At one of our conventions, I was so compelled to honor him. He may have never gotten the opportunity to speak time on stage, but while I was on stage, I called out to him, "Come up here, bro. Push us. Motivate the crowd. Do your thing."

Everyone matched his energy of enthusiasm the moment he stepped on stage. Not only did he have the time of his life because he had a great attitude, but he also impacted the lives of people who may never have met him. I know he touched my life because he made the most of what he was given.

There's no telling where that young man will be in the future because of his eagerness to take advantage of what was right in front of him. If we keep our eyes on the goal, we have more than what we need to fulfill our purpose.

TAKE RESPONSIBILITY

What happens if you want to stop making excuses? Well, you can't blame others. Instead, you have to be willing to accept accountability and take responsibility for your actions. The story of Adam, Eve, and the serpent in chapter three of Genesis perfectly illustrates how to play the blame game.

As the story goes, in Genesis chapter three, God commanded Adam and Eve not to eat fruit from a particular tree in the Garden of Eden. A nearby serpent tempted Eve and Adam to eat it, and the couple disobeyed the Lord. When God asked Adam whether they had eaten the forbidden fruit, Adam impetuously passed the blame to his wife. However, when Eve was confronted, she immediately passed the blame to the serpent.

Instead of blaming someone else for failure to reach your desired level, you have to take responsibility for where you are and look to where you want to go. It's not about where you start; it's about where you're going.

One of the most common momentum killers I've seen is the propensity to wait for someone else to act, take initiative, assume blame, or take charge. But very often, no help comes. Once you take responsibility, you may face two outcomes—stress or pressure.

PRESSURE YIELDS RESULTS

When I prepared to leave the Marine Corps, all the guys were dogging me out. They would say, "The only thing you know how to do is be a Marine. You'll be back in a month."

When I left, I didn't return. Contrary to their words, I made significant changes in order to work for myself and no one else. Some of my fellow Marines chose to remain in the same situation they were in when they joined. They played it safe because they felt the risks weren't worth the reward. Unfortunately, they have to live with their decision. We all do.

One of two things will happen when you make a decision. If you try to do things on your own—by your own strength—you'll end up stressed. On the other hand, when you operate and rely on your faith, you'll get pressure.

The Bible says, "We are hard pressed on every side, but not crushed; perplexed, but not in despair; persecuted, but not abandoned; struck down, but not destroyed" (2 Corinthians 4:8-9).

Many of us need standards, targets, and deadlines to push us towards good performance. Pressure is the need to perform, and everyone has an optimum level of pressure that brings about their best performance. The things I aim to achieve always come with pressure. I will work hard, take some risks, challenge myself, and change or accept new things—but it is manageable. Pressure helps me create a plan.

On the other hand, stress occurs when I stop focusing on who is in control. No matter how organized, effective, or efficient I am, I do not have the bandwidth to meet strenuous demands. The beauty (and benefits) of entrepreneurship is when you take risks and become your own boss. As a result, you reduce stress; however, you will face pressure.

Faith has equipped me to handle pressure because I know I can't do it alone. I learned to lean on God and trust that the right people will cross my path.

Stress hampers your ability to perform and causes a plethora of unnecessary issues. It reduces your creativity and productivity. Inauspiciously, several of the Marines I served with are still living stressful lives even after their enlistments were over. Their results differ from someone who has pressure because they are trying to control the outcome.

THE MISSION OF FAITH

God will help you with the boldness to ask for a promotion, but you have to open your mouth and speak. God will help you find a job, but you have to look and be ready for the interview. God will give you new ideas, but you have to be aware you can have the solution to people's problems.

God will help you improve your relationship with your spouse and kids, but you have to commit to spending time with them. God will help you pass the test, but you have to study. Let me put it in simpler terms: God's help does not remove your responsibility.

1. Persevere Through Your Pain Points

Mark 5:24-34 gives an account of a woman with an issue of blood. The unnamed woman in this Gospel story suffered for twelve years from a certain type of bleeding, often translated as hemorrhaging.

She visited many doctors and healers, and none of them could heal her. Finally, she heard Jesus Christ, known to heal many ill people, was passing through her town. She acted out in a last-ditch effort and slipped into the crowd, following Him.

In the past, society frowned upon her presence in public because of her illness. Neighbors skirted around her to avoid the possibility of contact; she lived in isolation and shame.

She knew she had taken a risk by stepping outside that day, but the solution to her problem was greater than her haven. Abandoning her comfort zone, she made her way through the crowd, hoping and praying for a touch of Jesus' garment. She believed that she would be healed if she at least touched it. Her arms reached over, and her fingers touched the garment, and God's power left it and healed her at once.

We can find ourselves waiting and praying when it may be time to start moving in faith. That is what the woman with the issue of blood did. In the end, Jesus said to her, "Your faith has healed you" (Luke 8:48).

Whether you're bleeding in your finances, marriage, or relationship with your kids, continue to persevere through the pain and lean on your faith. Nothing of value we desire comes without resistance. Perseverance is a testament that you fight for what you want.

2. Reap What You Sow

The law of seedtime and harvest is a process of exchange. If you desire to reap a harvest of any kind, you must sow the relevant seed. It is a simple but profound life principle. Farmers and the most successful people in the world grasp this concept. If the farmer wants to harvest maize, he sows maize seed. The more maize seed he sows, the more maize he can harvest. The more he harvests, the more he will reap.

Farmers implement the hunter-gatherer lifestyle. Although most Americans don't grow corn or hunt buffalo, this principle shows up in our careers, relationships, and businesses. You cannot reap a harvest where you have not sown seed. It's as simple as that.

However, if you plant in fertile ground, you could be a preacher or a thief and still yield a return. You can still have a harvest. Now, most believers don't want to hear that. But guess what? The thief can plant in good ground, the pastor can plant the same seed on cement, and the thief will get a harvest because he planted it in the right place.

If you want to have faith to move and do philanthropy, even if it's not in the local church, you are practicing that law. God's law is the law and it doesn't come back void (Isaiah 55:11). But regardless, if you're sowing, you have a responsibility to be sowing in good ground or taking opportunities to grow and improve.

When I flew missions in the Marine Corps, I'd see expensive mansions on the California coast. I'd always wonder how someone was able to afford that lifestyle and dreamed about buying one for myself one day. The costs of the houses blew me away when I purchased my first home twenty years ago. I found it odd that some of the pehole who owned mansions didn't believe in God, yet they benefited financially because they were following the laws of sowing and reaping. They were giving of their time, talents, and resources and were rewarded in return.

When it comes to finances, people with less money tend to view wealthy people as greedy and selfish. They believe that rich people cheat others in order to become wealthy. This is far from the truth. On the contrary wealthy people are the biggest givers and job creators in the world.

Proverbs 11:24 says, "There is one who scatters, yet increases more; and there is one who withholds more than is right, but it leads to poverty." To have good relationships, you need to be a good friend to other people. To better your skills in your profession, you must teach others what you know and learn from others to advance to a higher position. People who go into business dedicate an abundant amount of time and money to their ventures. As a result, they achieve financial freedom.

Whatever you want to receive, you must give. Unfortunately, we live in a corrupt world where most people tend to hold on to what they possess to get more. However, this is not how life works. Your investments will come back to you in a greater measure over time. As long as you live by this principle, your life will be a rich journey filled with peace and joy.

3. Help Yourself

Some people have the idea that faith is like a thermostat that works automatically. So, if we have faith when some great crisis comes, our faith should automatically turn on.

This thought process reminds me of a story of when Jesus calmed a storm (Matthew 8:23-27). Jesus and his disciples were crossing a sea, and a huge storm came upon them. The frantic disciples awakened Jesus because He was sleeping through it all. If faith worked automatically, it would have turned on when the storm blew up on the sea. Instead, Jesus arose and commanded the storm to cease, and it did. Then, Jesus rebuked them for their weak faith. They had the same ability as Him to calm the storm, yet they failed to *use* it.

God helps those who help themselves. In other words, if you apply faith in your life, you will get results. I can *believe* that my vehicle will take me wherever I want to go, but I practice faith by inserting the key into the ignition, then putting it in drive so that I can get from point A to point B. I can sit on top of that car all day long without the key in the ignition and say, "I believe. I believe. I believe." But if you say you believe, then you need to take the first step. You'll get more on your way than you do when you start.

4. Don't Overlook the Opportunity

On Sunday mornings, many people pray, "Lord, send me a financial miracle. Help me!" Of course, we are supposed to seek God when we need things, but it doesn't just stop there.

When you pray, the answer may be right in front of you, but you may not recognize it. If you don't see the opportunity for what it is, you'll accept the discounted version of what God is trying to accomplish in your life. God will send people, circumstances, and situations as signs to speak to you, but it might not necessarily be a burning bush, a booming voice from the heavens, or a parting of the Red Sea.

Instead of looking for a solution, you continue to have the same problem because you are waiting on God to answer your prayer the way you want Him to answer. When you do this, you can overlook what He has already given you.

If you ask anybody in our firm how they got started in life insurance—every one of them has a different answer. The reason why is because the insurance industry is not an industry that everyone aspirs to be part of as their first job. People happen to stumble across it as a third or fourth career.

Without knowing it, many who have taken this path have followed it through faith. It was better than the alternative—which was sitting at home and doing nothing. God makes a way even when you think there is no other way. Trusting this premise builds the strength and conviction of faith-made millionaires.

5. Pay Close Attention

You can change your life and the lives of those around you when you pay attention to how God orchestrates things in your life. He uses people and situations as signs to draw us into a deeper engagement of faith. It shows us how God is always active in our lives—if we allow Him to be. Unfortunately, we can miss out on these moments of enriching our relationship with our Creator and living the abundant life He desired for us to live.

I was working with an insurance marketing organization. Suddenly, they began to enforce regulations that prevented me from freely marketing myself on social media, according to corporate guidelines. Instead of being treated like an independent agent, I was treated like a glorified employee. That was when I knew I had to make a shift.

I looked for other opportunities. There were ten different options, including some with sign-on bonuses, but only one that had the same vision and mission as I did. The only company that asked me what I wanted was PHP Agency.

However, people around me warned me to avoid going into business with Patrick Bet-David. I didn't understand why. They never explained it clearly. However, the more people tell you *not* to do something, the more it makes you want to do it. So I had to take a faith step to see what would happen. I believe the results speak for themselves.

Plus, PHP Agency was acquired and created a strategic partnership with the biggest privately held company in the entire state of Texas. My wife and I were offered a handsome, mid-six-figure check to sell some of our stock, but we decided to roll one hundred percent of our equity ownership into the next bigger deal.

I wouldn't be where I am today if my wife hadn't prayed and encouraged me to faithfully seek why such negative energy was trying to keep us from going in this direction.

Had I listened to the people telling me what I needed to do instead of paying attention to the small signs God was giving me, I may have chosen another company.

For 430 years, Abraham's descendants, the Israelites, were enslaved in the land of Egypt by Pharaoh (Exodus 14). God sent Moses to tell Pharaoh to let God's people go, but Pharaoh said no. So God sent terrible plagues upon the country, proving His power and might.

After the last plague, Pharaoh summoned Moses and told him to leave Egypt. Then God told Moses, "I am going to lead you and the Israelites straight toward the Red Sea. I am going to put you in this impossible situation so that not only Israel but all of Egypt will know that I am the Lord God" (paraphrased).

Difficult situations do not happen by chance or by accident, but they're certainly not anything we would design for ourselves. Moses did not sit down with his map and say, "You know what? I want to plan a route that will ensure that we get trapped with absolutely no way of escape. So I am going to plan the most difficult route possible for the Israelites and me." It did not work that way then, and it surely doesn't work that way now.

We've all encountered difficult and impossible situations. But, I will never forget one I experienced. It was like any other day; I was heading to the office. I saw red and blue lights in my rear-view mirror. I looked down at my speedometer and realized I was going *slightly* over the speed limit. When I pulled over, I rolled the window down as the officer made his way to my car. After we briefly spoke, I handed him my license and registration. When he returned to his patrol car, I stared at my watch, noticing he was taking longer than the standard protocol.

When he finally approached my car to give me what I hoped was a warning, he informed me my license was suspended. *What?* I had no idea what he was talking about. By the grace of

God, he let me go and trusted that I would do the right thing. I started calling to see what was going on as quickly as possible.

A few calls later, I found out I had a $200k debt that had to be paid for me to get this situation resolved. Meanwhile, the state suspended my license without informing me. Instead of complaining or getting angry, I took action. I hired a lawyer, and after several court appearances, I won. Everything was dropped, and I didn't owe anything. Not only was a significant amount of money on the line, but my family, integrity, character, and the business I had built up to that point, were in jeopardy. My personal ignorance and manipulation from other parties got me in the situation. It seemed insurmountable, but I had faith and did my part. Thankfully, it ended in my favor.

Looking back, anything could have happened. There was no way I would have known what the outcome was going to be, but I trusted God and did my part.

So, while God may not part the actual Red Sea and say, "Okay, come on through now. This is your opportunity. This is your miracle." He will provide a way of escape when you are in difficult situations. He will put you in positions where you will only be able to rely on Him, and you will know without a shadow of a doubt He brought you out of the situation.

Faith-made millionaires don't have everything planned out. They move forward, equipped with their current knowledge, surrounded by trusted advisors, and allow the Big Man Upstairs to have a supernatural effect on their endeavors.

In the next chapter, I'll break down some concepts of fear and how you can use it to push you forward instead of allowing it to hinder you. If we aren't careful, we can respond as the disciples did during the storm. The trials in our lives reveal how much faith we have and how much we need. If your first thought in a difficult situation is fear, then you need to assess where you put your faith and how you can trust God because you may be in charge, but you aren't in control.

3

Reject the Spirit of Fear

"Fear is a self-imposed prison that will keep you from becoming what God intends for you to be."

—Rick Warren

I grew up in the Berwyn, Stickney, and Cicero area of Chicago, formerly known as the Al Capone territory next to two horse tracks, so I spent a lot of time there. I'd always study the horses when I went to the races. After all, I wanted to have the best chance of knowing which one would win. So I'd read the guides and learn about who the jockey was.

How I knew to research at a young age blows my mind, but it has paid off in the long run. Then I learned the most critical factors for a winning horse: it was not about the jockey or the breed of horse; it was when and what they ate before the race, which reminds me of a story I heard.

One day, a father and his son walked through a horse stable.

The son looked up to his dad and asked, "Which horses will race at the Kentucky Derby tomorrow?"

The dad replied, "I have one named Faith and one named Fear. They will run the race."

"Yeah, Dad. Awesome. Well, which one is going to win?"

"Well, Son, the one that is going to win today is the one I decide to feed."

FEEDING FEAR OR FAITH

Whatever you look for, you'll find because what you focus on magnifies. So, for example, if you want to find ways to feed your faith, you will find a bunch of YouTube content, books, and websites that will inspire and motivate you.

If you want to find things that feed your fear, skepticism, and criticism, you will find them. *The Social Dilemma*, a documentary released in 2020, exposes how social media can open the door to feeding fear in our lives.

In the documentary, former employees of today's largest social media companies reveal how their networks track what you click on the most. Then their algorithms will pick up on it and send you curated ads. If they can keep your eyes on that platform to feed whatever you're clicking on, they have more opportunities to sell you. The lesson is that you will get more of what you're viewing—online or in real life.

Fear and faith have their own algorithm; without you knowing it, you are subconsciously doing the same thing as the algorithms for social media. Subsequently, you are steadily grabbing more and more things that align with your current thoughts.

If you want a different thought, you have to rewire your brain to things that will benefit you. You can only do this by changing what you view and listen to.

We hinder much of our success because we realize it requires work. Forget taking a leap of faith–we don't want to even take a faith step. If you're going to accomplish something big in life, will you feed faith or fear? Before eliminating fear, you need to know what fear looks like and recognize how it shows up in your life.

The term "spirit of fear" comes from 2 Timothy 1:7: "For God hath not given us the spirit of fear; but of power, and of love, and of a sound mind" (King James Version). When I decided to live for God, God replaced the spirit of fear in me with the spirit of faith. It was not instantaneous but a journey of obedience and discipline to Him.

The truth is most people fail to see they're operating in fear because it's so normal. It might manifest in different ways than one might expect. For example, have you ever been paralyzed by a decision? What is the right course to take? What will happen if you make the wrong choice? Fear immobilizes us; we contemplate what could happen if we make a mistake. However, the fear inside us often makes the consequences or problems seem much more earth-shattering than they truly are.

All of this certainty comes from failing to put our trust completely in God. Instead, we must trust that no matter what happens, even if we make the wrong choice, God still holds on to us. He is always with us, no matter what path we take.

When making decisions, we should remember Psalm 119:105, "Your word is a lamp for my feet, a light on my path," and James 1:5, "If any of you lacks wisdom, you should ask God, who gives generously to all without finding fault, and it will be given to you." These promises are my anchor when I am tempted to fear. So make sure you are feeding the right horse.

FIVE INDICATORS OF FEAR

You may not see yourself as a "fearful" person, but fear shows up in several subtle ways. It can be avoiding anything with the possibility of failure, embarrassment, rejection, or worrying about the future, and anticipating the worst. It can be a sense of having to defend yourself constantly. The bottom line of this pervasive, non-functional fear is that it keeps you from being, doing, and having what you want. Throughout my life, I have identified five ways fear attempts to show up.

1. Perfectionism

You control your life by what you can do and how you might fail. It's scary to think about rejection or not being good enough; if these thoughts rule your head, then so will fear. It's good to try as hard as possible to do things will excellence, but it's unhealthy to be a perfectionist. Your life will be controlled by what you cannot do, how you might fail. Pride and ego can show up because you can get to a place where you think no one can do things as good as you.

2. Procrastination

You have priorities; these can be easy tasks or much harder ones. If you love to procrastinate most of the time, you could be lazy. Then again, you could also be living in fear.

Some of these things you need to do will take courage, and you know this. Hence, it's the reason you put it off for another day. The truth is, it's best to get it done and move on. However, that's much easier said than done.

3. Overcommitment

We tend to commit to things that were never meant to be permanent. It could be a relationship, a place to live, or a job. Now, we can't see a way out. So we overcommit to give ourselves that feeling of stability. It helps quell our fears. But we get trapped in places we were never meant to stay.

When I started serving the church more regularly, I found myself at church every day participating in ministry activities. Due to this, I drifted from my first ministry and responsibility, which was serving my family and the business God sent my way to build. I learned that saying "yes" was very expensive, and there was more freedom to say "no" so I could focus on what matters most.

4. Settling for Less

Fear can cause us to shrink back from our dreams and aspirations. Fear is the tiny voice that whispers, "You could never do that. You aren't smart enough. You aren't talented enough. You aren't qualified enough. It will take too long. It won't happen for you."

5. Guilt and Shame

Another reason why people fear success is because of guilt. They make more money than their parents, extended family, friends, and everybody from their past. So now they feel guilty because they drive a nicer car and live in an upper-income neighborhood.

I often run across this in people we coach in starting their business in the insurance industry. I see them plateau in their income because they don't know how to handle the people they grew up with asking for money. Once they break through this by creating a system for lending money, they realize how much of a greater inspiration and financial blessing they can give to those who need jobs. They find themselves investing more deeply into their communities in a much larger capacity.

I had to work through the guilt of other people's expectations, leaving people behind, and feeling bad about not giving people money just because I had money.

HOW TO OVERCOME FEAR

Now that you've identified some of the symptoms of fear take the next step and overcome! If you know what you want and run after it, you will achieve far more in your life.

Take Risks

We love the thought of being financially free. We romance about being great contributors to our communities and desire to serve the poor and help the needy. However, greatness comes with a hefty price tag—and that is taking risks.

Over the years, I've talked to so many people about personal financing and entrepreneurship. They dream of a different life and resent where they are. They listen for a few minutes, but then the spirit of fear kicks in, and their hearts harden. When I check in a year later, their lives are still the same. Five years later, it's only five percent better.

One day, I parked my car at the gym, and a couple of kids surrounded my car.

"What's up? Can I help you, kids?" I said, slowly opening my car door.

One boy asked, "Are you the MoneySmartGuy?"

"Yep," I said—wondering how they knew who I was.

"I follow your YouTube channel," he said and looked at his friends. "Well, we all follow your YouTube channel."

"What are you doing following an *old* man's YouTube channel?" I jokingly asked.

"Are you kidding?" He responded. "We want to make money."

After talking to them, I discovered I had talked to their parents years ago about coming onboard with PHP Agency. Their parents had their own thoughts about how they viewed money and what risks they would take. I believe fear motivated their decisions.

I hope the kids following me on social media plan to learn more about finances and business so they can edcuate themselves to take calculated risks as they get older, even if they don't have the immediate support of their families.

Step Out of Your Comfort Zone

Stepping out of your comfort zone is the key to breaking the stagnancy in your life. Any time you do something you normally wouldn't, you're flexing your break-free muscle and getting more comfortable with risk-taking. So when is the last time you've stepped outside your comfort zone? When you're stretching beyond your usual limits, it helps reinforce the idea that you're capable of enduring new challenges. And that feeling, in turn, can make the original goal a little less intimidating. Feed faith, and you will have the strength to overcome!

Understand Fear is Not Real

As you keep pressing on, always keep an eye on potential fears desiring to creep back in and drive our life choices. In the movie,

After Earth, starring Will Smith, aliens ravaged the earth. The aliens carry the ability to sense fear and use it against humans. By rejecting the feeling of fear, the characters turned invisible as they walked among the aliens.

In our lives, we must do the same thing when fear tries to creep into our minds. In the movie, Will Smith said, "Fear is not real. The only place that fear can exist is in our thoughts of the future. It is the product of our imagination, causing us to fear things that do not at present and may not ever exist."

When you deconstruct fear, you begin to see it's not real. It is all in our minds based on our thoughts and feelings about events that may or may not ever happen.

Not real means it can't be physically seen; you can't say that one thing is the source of fear because that is different for everyone. For example, one person might be terrified of heights while another loves it and enjoys the adrenaline they get when looking down from the top floor of a building.

Fear only exists in the minds of people who choose to experience it. Thankfully, we carry the power to choose how we react and view the world, and fear is one of the things. Trust me, it's not easy to control and expel your fear, but it's certainly possible.

It is one of those basic emotions that has become so pervasive it's almost like the air many people breathe. It's based on things from the past that hasn't been released. It is focused on threats and dangers that aren't real—or if "real," not as serious as the fear would have us believe.

What can we do to fight off fear? On our own, we *should* fear. We have no control over the world. We don't control people, circumstances, or the weather as much as we may try to prepare for every possibility.

However, God *does* have complete control. He also knows exactly what is going to happen. Therefore, the only way to fight fear is to put our trust in Him. Consider 1 John 4:18: "There is no fear in love. But perfect love drives out fear." God's love is perfect. Knowing that He loves us, we can easily abandon fear.

4

Family Matters

"Family is the compass that guides us.
They are the inspiration to reach great heights
and our comfort when we occasionally falter."
— **Brad Henry**

The family is the bedrock of a healthy society and it always begins with a solid marriage. Family is about multiple people contributing to one story. In truth, we are part of a bigger narrative. Our story is never jut about ourselves. Family is about recognizing how we impact others and how others have shaped us.

Marriage is a covenant of love and commitment—a loving, intimate, selfless relationship between a man and a woman. In Malachi 2:14, marriage is described as a holy covenant before God. It is *so* much more than a civil contract with legal benefits. It is an essential part of God's plan.

Who you marry is one of the most significant decisions of your life—as well as who you have kids with. Believe me, I know firsthand the menacing cost of making the wrong decision.

As I've mentioned, I was previously married, yet it ended in divorce. Like David, Solomon, and Samson, I got caught in the moment and let physical attraction and lust overshadow my discernment and decisions. Ladies and gents, it's crucial to follow what my mentor, Patrick Bet David says, "Fall in love emotionally, but marry logically." Although I learned the hard way, I have since discovered marriage must-haves to have a lasting marriage.

SIX MARRIAGE MUST-HAVES

A good marriage partner is one of the foundations for a thriving family. Here are six qualities I recommend you look for in your future spouse. If you are already married, work together to come together in agreement with these points.

1. Respect Beliefs and Values

The person you marry doesn't have to agree with you on every issue, but even so, you must have mutual respect for each other's core beliefs and values. It is even better when you share the same ones because it makes it easier to stay on the same page. How could it be possible to keep loving a person you don't respect or are in constant conflict with? (Spoiler alert: It's not.)

2. Growth

The person you marry should help you evolve into a better version of yourself. That doesn't mean they should belittle you with insults or tell you that you're not good enough because positive transformation cannot and will not happen without total acceptance of who you are. On the other hand, your partner should challenge you to step up your game in every aspect of your life.

3. Compromise

The person you marry shouldn't be a weak-willed pushover who bends to your every whim, but it also doesn't mean they can be stubborn. One person in the relationship is rarely 100% right or wrong in any given argument. The answer usually lies somewhere in the middle.

Your partner should be willing to talk through any given issue with you and know how to compromise with you.

4. Accept Responsibility

The person you marry doesn't have to be perfect, but they should be truthful enough to admit it when they are wrong. It is okay to make a mistake as long as a sincere apology, and honest explanation follow it. But suppose your partner avoids all conflict, denies all shortcomings, and is unwilling to apologize. In that case, you might want to consider having the hard conversations so you can address your concerns—or you could be facing a constant storm of marital strife which doesn't sound like fun.

5. Share Future Vision

The person you marry doesn't have to be on the same life path as you, but your trials should converge in enough places to reach your final destination together. In other words, you might have a slight problem if you want to travel overseas, but your partner is too scared to even get on the plane. Different viewpoints on wealth and how to rear your children can be big points of contention.

The sooner you know and talk about this early in the relationship, the better. They may not be the person you need to marry. The last thing you want to do is hinder them from what they desire or allow them to get in the way of your dreams and goals.

6. Embrace Change

The person you marry shouldn't resist change with every ounce of their being. Sometimes life presents us with open doors of opportunity that could lead to a new career, a house, a hometown, or (insert the limitless possibilities that could occur here). If you love to improvise based on the contents of the hand you're dealt, no matter where that might take you, then you shouldn't settle down with a rigid partner who is so afraid of change that they won't even discuss the issue with you.

Notice that sex isn't ranked very high. I think once you get over the lustful, groggy sex, you'll realize that there is more to getting along than multiple orgasms or sexual positions. Sure, you need to be physically attracted to one another, but over time, this begins to wither away. You'll now have to deal with the character of the person you chose to marry. When you discover intimacy in your sex life, it's much easier to do life with the other person.

LOVE AND RESPECT

Study these six must-haves and keep them in mind as you go about your life looking for a spouse. Then, when you choose the right person to live your life with, you are ready to start a family. If you're already married, make sure both of you are on the same page. Trust me, it makes all the difference. I'm including a QR code so you can watch the interview I did on marriage to dive in a bit deeper on the subject.

The parents' primary responsibility in the family is to instill priceless values and principles in their children. I grew up in a home where my parents were together, blissfully ignorant of our financial situation or the challenges of immigrant parents. As a result, I never grasped the magnitude of a family until I had one of my own.

I learned more about my father from how his friends and co-workers respected him. They would tell me how he admired me, and I wondered why my Dad never said it to me directly. I would later realize that he had childhood trauma growing up during World War II and the bombing of Manila. My aunt would tell me how she would teach him how to "play dead" in the streets as the Japanese soldiers with fixed bayonets would kill any moving thing. My father was raised by a single father, and no one in our family talks about how my grandmother died.

As I have grown as a parent, I often reflect on my relationship with my father. In many ways, he was present in my life. But in other ways, he was absent. I wish we would have talked more, but we didn't—just like there are times I should have shown him more appreciation, but I didn't. There are games I wished he would have attended, but he couldn't be there. I'd look for him in the stands, but he didn't show up. I'm sure there was a list of things he would have liked from me too.

I remember him being at one of my freshman games, but after that game, I didn't see him for the remainder of my high school years. I held that against him for a while. I believe we missed out on conversations about life that could have helped me make better choices, but now that I'm a dad, I know he did the best with what he knew. That's all any parent can do.

Growing up, I went through three phases in regards to how I viewed my father. Then, when I came to faith, I experienced them with my Heavenly Father. As a father, I can see what it's like to be on the other side.

Phase 1: Idolize

As kids grow up, their father becomes their first hero. Kids give their fathers the utmost praise and respect. On the playground, kids say, "My dad's stronger than you. My dad's faster than you. My dad's richer than you."

The same thing happens when you first come to faith. We praise God and spend time in awe of what has happened in your life and how you have been able to get through certain situations.

Phase 2: Demonize

This phase typically happens in the teenage to young adult years. You think your father doesn't know anything about you, or they are always against you. You may say things like, "I can't do anything right. You're always disciplining me." You may even question why you can't do certain things and believe he's out to make your life miserable.

This can also happen with our Heavenly Father. When we go through a difficult time, we may question where God is and why certain things happened to us. It can be seen as demonizing because we believe God wasn't there for us, so we question why we should follow our faith at all.

Phase 3: Humanize

Humanizing is the third and final phase. Since I've grown up and somewhat matured, I've humanized my father. I realized how much he endured as a child and how he grew up gravely affected him.

There is no way I could imagine putting my children to sleep and telling them to pretend to play dead. My three-year-old right now can't stop wiggling when I carry him from the house to the car.

My father endured trauma during his childhood—as we all do. Not only that, but he was also raised by a single father and came to America, where he didn't know anybody. Looking back, I can see how difficult that must have been.

He had to find his way around an unfamiliar city to get jobs and a place to live. Learning about his history made me realize why my dad made me do certain things a certain way. Through his story, he taught me empathy and gratitude. I was remorseful for resenting him because I never considered what he experienced. There were times I was extremely difficult, and I knew better. I didn't understand things from his perspective. I only viewed things from a lens of selfishness.

My father and I have the chance to spend time together now. We get along and have built a relationship with this next chapter in life. So he may not have been at my games as a kid, but he can see me as a man, take a tour of my office, and witness the legacy I'm building. I hope he can see the morals and values he instilled in me being lived out.

LEAD BY EXAMPLE

Proverbs 22:6 says, "Train up a child in the way he should go: and when he is old, he will not depart from it." The ultimate goal as a parent is to lay a foundation so their children will be an asset to society and care for themselves when they become adults. That is the goal, though parents cannot force children to make the right decisions—the same way God does not force us to make the right decisions. He will lead and direct us, but He gives us the freedom to make our own decisions.

Not all have been privileged to experience a pattern of consistency in parenting, but we experience consistency through God. The Bible states that the Creator of the universe operates on the "blessing for obedience and correction for disobedience" principle (Leviticus 26). If we follow this principle consistently in parenting, we lay the foundation for the future.

Our personal example is of the utmost importance! Children must see their parents living out our values and principles daily. The parent's example primarily develops children's perception of God. Suppose they see intolerance, hypocrisy, self-centeredness, poor stewardship, and frequent anger. In that case, they will not likely be attracted to their parents' belief system and go against their values or pick up the poor habits and generational curses.

As much as I want to discipline my children and raise my family based on telling them what to do or writing down what I thought via text, email, letters, or cards, I realized they followed more what I *did* than what I said. They didn't learn values on money, marriage, life, and business when I told them about it but rather by me living it out.

More is Caught Than Taught

When my children were younger, we used to commute a lot in Chicago, back and forth to different activities, school, and my appointments. My son would hear me talk to potential clients, customers, and my business partners on the phone via Bluetooth or speaker phone in the car. As a result, he quickly learned how to sell. My son has the gift of gab. He can sell himself into a job. He knows how to sell any product or service he's passionate about.

If there's one thing I've always told my kids to learn and master, it would be to master the ability to sell because sales will help you in a myriad of ways. It will help you become a better communicator, stand firmly on your beliefs, and strengthen your thoughts and ideas, so others listen to you. So not only did I tell them, I showed them.

Instill Integrity

My parents drilled in me the importance of being a man of my word. To this day, I credit my mom and dad for their lessons on integrity. Through mimicry, integrity has become a strong point in my life. Having integrity shows your heart, and it's vital for every relationship.

Think about this process of mimicry and completion, and now think about your children. What are the things you want them to mimic to help them succeed in their lives? Now think of ways you can live that out. Again, it goes back to the Sapaula Family Values I shared in chapter two. I don't want my kids just to do what I say; I want them to see why they need to do it.

Set the tone for your children. My twins learned when I was in business mode because I prospected the servers every time we went out to eat. Now my children know how to make new friends and don't feel indifferent when in a crowd of people who don't look like them. My kids later revealed to me that they watched what I did. I was unaware that they noticed until I saw them doing it as they got older.

Kids will find someone to follow if you're not setting an example at home. Sometimes it will be in a positive light, and other times, it may not be so positive. As much as you think you're improving your kids, your kids will end up causing you to improve yourself.

Ask yourself if you want your kids to look up to other people or you. It's less about what you say and more about what you do. Our words and actions have power when working together.

Include the Family

I integrate my kids into my daily activities and meetings. They are part of our trips, conventions, and events. They see their dad speak on stage and conduct meetings behind closed doors. They see me shaking hands with powerful and influential people in a much different financial stratosphere than I am currently in.

I want them to see me at my best because when they want to chase after their dreams and goals, they'll have an example to follow. What I have—consciously and subconsciously instilled in them is a work habit and a work ethic and to love people and treat them with respect.

As parents, we must pour into our children and teach them things we never learned growing up. For instance, I have dialogue around money and teach them how to use finances properly instead of having our kids wake up with a bucket full of cash. If not addressed and handled correctly, they will be like Richie Rich and won't know how to handle money.

As I read my favorite two books in the Bible, which are Proverbs and Ecclesiastes, the main principles I've learned to obtain wealth the *right* way are:

- Be diligent with your work and despise laziness.
- Embrace discipline and walk in integrity.
- Seek wisdom and the right associations.

Teach your kids this, and they will learn the value of hard work and enjoy the fruit of their labor!

Set Children Up for Success

Something we constantly talk about in my family is having answers for the most demanding challenges life will throw at you.

Families need constant communication, and children need their parents to discuss real-life scenarios. For example, I often ask them if they want to attend college or join the military. They know they have options, including entrepreneurship. However, I want them to consider the outcome of whatever their decision may be.

I always ask my kids: Will going to college to get your desired job justify the debt? What is the outcome of going to college? I want my children to avoid the life-altering burden of student-loan debt.

They were like me when it came to being athletically gifted—we were good enough to make the team but not good enough to further our careers as athletes. They lacked interest in STEM, science, technology, education, engineering, and math. So, they chose to forgo college. I would be more than happy to assist them if they wanted to attend college. I would pay half, and they would be responsible for the other half.

I remember taking my daughters to Hawaii on an all-expensive company-paid trip. We were relaxing and soaking in the moment.

I took them on one-on-one dates so I could speak with them individually. I asked, "What do you want to do?"

"I want to get in the insurance industry."

"That's great," I said. "Why do you want to do insurance?"

"Papi, look at us," one of my daughters said. "We're here. We're in Hawaii on the beach. The moon is looking at us. The waves are crashing right next to us. What job could do all this? I love this! I want to do insurance."

The same one who said this became a licensed life insurance agent. Now it's a bit early to tell, but we will see whether or not she will follow in Daddy's footsteps. They can only ride on my coattail for so long before they have to do their own thing. But then again, all I can do is show them what life has to offer and let them decide what they want to do.

PURSUE YOUR DREAMS GUILT-FREE

It's common for entrepreneurs to feel they need to choose between their personal and professional lives, but you don't have to. As a CEO, husband, and father, I spend a lot of time reflecting on this dynamic.

Why are we led to believe that we must make familial sacrifices to succeed as entrepreneurs or vice versa? Are we not able to nurture our family life while simultaneously embracing our careers? It may be demanding, but it's possible.

Willing to Pay the Price

Sadly, most people underestimate the effort and reality it takes to improve their families situation. That causes guilt in many marriages. In addition, it creates guilt for parents because they have to invest time away from their kids at some moments. So instead of having a guilt trip for not being at dinner every night, I am willing to pay the price. As a reward, I can take my family on a trip around the world and help them establish their future.

When I got serious about my finances and changing the trajectory for my family, I paid the price of not going to parties or staying late at events. I would rather be studying late at night instead of drinking and ending up with a hangover that would impact my productivity the following day. If you aren't willing to the pay the price now, you will pay for it later.

Realistic Balance

"I need to find balance in my life and family." If you've ever found yourself saying those things, the reality is that if you weren't raised with a wealthy family or given an inheritance, your family is already out of balance. I say that because unless you are a business owner or entrepreneur, you spend most of your time working for other people. Then, without even knowing it, you're just happy to have what your boss gives you. Or you're just content with any free time you have leftto spend with the people you love and care about and raise your kids.

Let Go of Self-Condemnation

The pull of providing for your family while also desperately wanting to be a good husband and parent is challenging. I can't be at everything; however, there isn't a day that goes by that my children have to question if I love them.

One of the ways I have let go of guilt is by having a wife who understands the assignment. We partner together to make things happen. When she married me, she knew I wouldn't be the husband who would be home by five o'clock every night, eat dinner with the kids, watch TV, and work on the kids' schoolwork or activities every evening. My wife and I are a team. We create and live by a schedule, so I don't experience guilt for not being at all the practices or all their games.

I have created goals and aspirations to accomplish for my family. I wanted to live comfortably and a lifestyle of financial freedom. I knew what I had to do to live in a certain neighborhood, provide my kids with an excellent education, and have a reliable network. Power and control over our lives require more time and effort to develop.

Negotiate Your Time

People can feel guilty because they have to miss their kids' events. I totally get it. That's why you must learn how to master the negotiation of time. You must attend some events and others you will need to miss to establish a different financial reality for the next generation. Therefore, they do not have to divide as much time between their career and family when they grow up.

POWER OF A LAST NAME

Roughly twenty years ago, I hired a marketing consultant to help choose a brand and a name for my firm. After a short conversation, she led me through this exercise by asking some questions.

Her first question was, "If you were going to buy something of high value to gift someone, where would you go shopping?"

Without hesitation, I said, "I would go to the mall—Neiman Marcus or Nordstrom's. Then I'd buy Gucci or Versace. I'd buy something name-brand if it were for a special occasion."

Her next question was, "What type of cars do you like?"

"Lamborghinis, Ferraris, Mercedes, and Rolls Royce."

"Well, what about watches?"

"Rolex and Patek Philippe."

As we went through the exercise, she asked if I noticed any patterns or what each of these things had in common. She explained that every brand I said was someone's last name. Years ago, one family member decided to create something of value. They invested their lifetime in building a company and reputation, invoking respect. Due to this, they are high luxury items that only the majority of the elite and wealthy wear and own.

The Rockefeller, Kennedy, Walton and Trump families all emphasize the importance of generational wealth and giving back. We had former President George W. Bush one year at our annual convention. I learned that the Bush family instilled into their children the values of attending Yale University and building a career to provide for themselves. Once they did that, they could get married and begin bearing children. You take care of yourself, then your wife and kids—in that order. Then moving forward, you contribute the rest of your life to public service.

One family that built a fortune by helping shape America was the Vanderbilts. Cornelius Commodore Vanderbilt built the steamboats that transported everything in America, from east to west. He sold that business and created the railroad system in America. By his death in 1877, he amassed a $100M fortune, which, adjusted for inflation, would be worth over $2.7B today.[3]

Sadly, by the fourth generation, the family fortune was all gone. Reginald and his brother Cornelius III were avid gamblers and spent tons of money on high society appearances. Reginald was father to fashion designer Gloria Vanderbilt and grandfather to CNN anchor Anderson Cooper.

When the Vanderbilts held a family reunion at Vanderbilt University in 1973 with 120 family members, not one was a millionaire. I believe one of the reasons why they don't have

---

[3]Peter Churchouse, Stansberry Churchouse Research Dec 17, 2017,How one of the richest dynasties in American history lost its fortune

generational wealth is because they stopped educating their children about financial discipline. They didn't talk about protecting and growing their wealth.

Gloria Vanderbilt and Anderson Cooper are the only Vanderbilt with wealth that we see today that's prominent in pop culture in our world. However, what do we see with the Rockefeller family? They are the most affluent family still on the Forbes 500 List. The Walton family is still on the Forbes 500 List. Because these families contributed to society, gave back, and created wealth. They built their last name to last.

Why do these people have certain lifestyles? Why do certain people travel around the world? Why do these people live in private neighborhoods? Why do people have these opportunities? Because someone understood the power they could have and went after it.

They made the decision a long time ago, generations beforehand, and declared that their family would be changed by their choices. The current generation may not make a massive impact. Nor will the next or third, but four or five generations later, a massive impact will be made.

I want to do this for my family, along with more multicultural families. Filipinos didn't come into the United States until the 1960s, but that doesn't mean I can't make the change with my children's generation. It only takes one person in a family's bloodline to change their last name forever.

As I close this chapter, I have a few questions for you:

- What last name are you creating?
- What do you want your family legacy to be?
- How important is it for your great, great-grandkids to know your name?

As you go into the next section of the book, I want you to keep an open mind. The finance section will include and break down a lot of information—so don't rush through it. But don't worry, I've simplified it so that it's easy enough for a fifth grader to understand.

PILLAR II

FINANCES

"Do you know why God wants you rich? So you can do more. The wealthier you become, the more responsible you are to God."

—Jerry Savelle

5

Don't Bury Your Talents

"*Your talent is God's gift to you.*
What you do with it is your gift back to God."
— **Leo Buscaglia**

One evening, I headed toward an ATM, frustrated because I doubted I had had twenty dollars to withdraw to feed my kids. As I was about to insert my card, I saw a receipt from the person who used the machine before I did. Looking around, I didn't see anyone. So, I curiously grabbed the receipt before making my withdrawal. I read it. When my eyes focused on the numbers, my jaw almost touched the ground. Here I am looking only to get the bare minimum of twenty dollars. Yet this receipt showed that someone before just withdrew the daily maximum of $500.

Not only that, the remaining balance had more money than I ever had at one time, which made the sting of being broke even worse. In fact, I had never known anyone to have that much money sitting in a checking account. So, if you were the one who left their receipt in the ATM in the Western Springs Dominick's grocery store, circa 2003, God used you to change my life.

For those who are just as curious as I was, here's a picture of the receipt to see the amount for yourself. To this day, it serves as a bookmark in my Bible and a daily reminder to be humble, grateful, and curious.

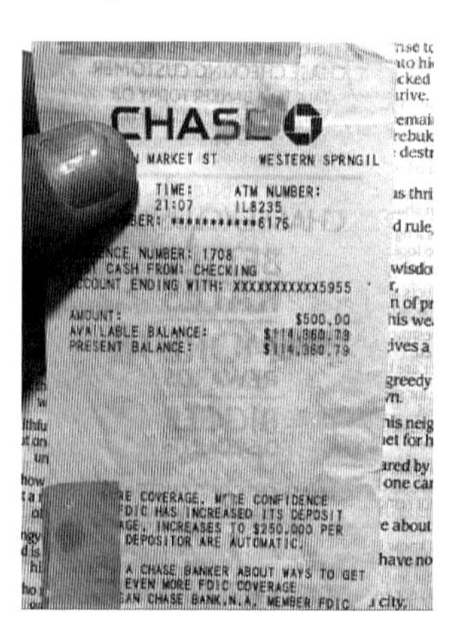

Yes, you are seeing that correctly! The account had over $114k in it. My account rarely had a balance with more than three figures. God's sense of humor caught me off guard. The valuable lesson God showed me was not everyone was living paycheck-to-paycheck. Not everyone lived in lack. This person withdrew the highest daily limit possible, while I was anxious to withdraw the minimum.

I thanked God I could get twenty dollars out of the ATM and headed home. God sparked something in me that I hadn't felt before. I wanted to learn how people could live above average—without stress or worry about their finances. It gave me a glimpse that people around me were living comfortably financially. I was determined to find out what they knew about money that I didn't.

The ATM receipt became a paradigm shift that will impact future generations. I used the discouragement to fuel my determination so I could strive for more. I went home and started reading the Bible after dinner and putting the kids to bed. I didn't have a particular verse in mind. I had been praying for God to show me what I could do to live that way—not to be wealthy but to learn how to manage my money.

Looking at the receipt in front of me, I thumbed through the Bible and stopped in Matthew. The first chapter I saw was Matthew chapter twenty-five, so I began reading. It was Jesus telling the Parable of the Talents.

To paraphrase, the master was leaving for a journey and assembled his three servants. Then he gave them talents (or money) according to their ability. Yes, according to their *ability*. I believe their ability was based on their experience and trustworthiness of being able to deliver on previous tasks.

The first one received five, the second received two, and the third one received one. Then, after giving the talents away, the master left on a long journey.

After the master returned from his long journey, he checked in with his servants to see what they accomplished with their talents while he was away. The first two doubled their talents. He was very pleased with the results of their actions.

Then he turned his attention to the servant who had been given one talent. The master asked what he did with his talents. The third servant's response was he *knew* his master was harsh, so he buried them to keep them safe. Out of fear, he did nothing the entire time the master was gone.

THREE LESSONS FROM THE BIBLE THAT MADE ME MILLIONS

The master's response was rather harsh—at least, I thought so at the time. First, he informed him he could have at least put it in the bank to earn some interest. Then, he dismissed and kicked him out of his estate by calling him a filthy and wicked servant. Each time I read this story, I learned something new to implement. Until then, I had always wondered if savings and investing are biblical—*it is.* I had been going to church for several years, but I had not heard of any pastor or spiritual teaching about the subject of personal finances so I wondered if I should be saving and investing.

THIS BIBLE STORY MADE ME MILLIONS

If I didn't have any money to invest—I needed to know why I was *still* living paycheck to paycheck. I had so many questions, so I began breaking the story down.

1. God Expects a Return

Most people are tempted to feel sorry for the servant who received only one talent, but in reality, he received a significant amount of money. Then he went and buried it in his backyard. Have you ever wondered what a talent is worth in today's economy? It is hard to know for sure, yet whatever its exact value, in the New Testament, a *talent* indicates a large sum of money. I am no mathematician, but some scholars guesstimate that one talent weighed seventy-five pounds. Based on what silver is worth in 2022, that would be equivalent to roughly $20,650, give or take.

I felt sorry for him before I realized he was given more than enough to meet the master's expectations. After all, he was given anywhere close to $20k, that's how much I was making in an entire year. I had to earn it, but he was given that much and didn't do anything with it.

Just as the master expected his servants to do more than preserve what has been entrusted to them, God expects us to generate a return by using our talents. The servants were given enough to produce. It is the same with the gifts God has given us. Apostle Paul writes in Ephesians 2:10, "For we are God's handiwork, created in Christ Jesus to do good works, which God prepared in advance for us to do." Ask yourself if you are making the most of your talents. If you are, you should see a return. If you aren't seeing a return, you may need to reevaluate what your talents are and how you can use them.

2. God Gives Based on Our Ability

The most overlooked part of this parable is the second half of verse fifteen: the master gives each servant talents "...each according to his ability." The master understood that the one-talent servant could not produce as much as the five-talent servant.

We want to protest this as unfair. (Spoiler alert: life isn't fair.) Yet we know this is true from our own experience. Diversity is woven into the fabric of creation.

Although we're not created equal regarding our talents, there *is* equality found in the Parable of the Talents. It comes from the fact that it takes just as much work for the servant who was given five talents to produce five more talents as the servant who was given two talents to create two more.

This is why the reward given by the master is the same—the master measures success by degrees of effort and ability. Talents could also be the talents of singing, engineering, math, sales—whatever talent that has been given and developed. I wonder what these servants were doing with their time. After all, they were living on the master's estate and exposed to the same things to increase their ability so surely they knew what to do with an opportunity when it came their way.

3. God Provides Opportunity

The Parable of the Talents teaches us what we are supposed to do. We are to work, using our talents to serve the common good and further God's kingdom. Biblical success is working diligently in the here and now, using all the talents God has given us to produce the return expected by the master.

Scripture enjoins us to pay attention to financial matters (Proverbs 27:23-24). While God provides for the birds, He doesn't plop the worms in their mouths as they sit in their nests!

They have to exert some effort to obtain the worms that God has provided. They have to search, hunt, dig, extract and then eat.

The unfaithful steward in this parable didn't so much waste the master's money–he wasted an opportunity. As a result, he was judged. We are responsible for what we do for God with what we have been given, and we are held accountable based on what we do with the opportunities we receive.

What do you do with the opportunities you have been given? I almost forfeited the opportunity that blessed me to become the faith-made millionaire that I am today.

When I started in the insurance industry, I happened to go to California, around the same time my sister, Jocelyn had just started working at a church. She wanted to introduce me Pastor Dudley Rutherford, so I agreed. When we met, he told me I reminded him of someone that I needed to meet. He said we had three things in common: 1) he was in the service, 2) he was an immigrant, and 3) he also worked in finances.

I thought of it as nothing more than a coincidence. Then, without knowing it, Pastor Dudley happened to go to the person I reminded him of and told him the same thing about me. He was adamant about us connecting, but I didn't think anything of it.

It was not too longer after this conversation that I received a message on Facebook. It appeared the commonalities that Pastor Dudley shared peaked his interested and he thought it would be great to have a conversation.

You can check out the message for yourself. This message happened to be sent in 2009 and was none other than Patrick Bet-David. The sad thing was, I blew him off. It was years later before we connected and I brought my business to PHP Agency. Initially, I didn't acknowledge the opportunity because I was adamant about doing things my way and was still operating from fear and scarcity.

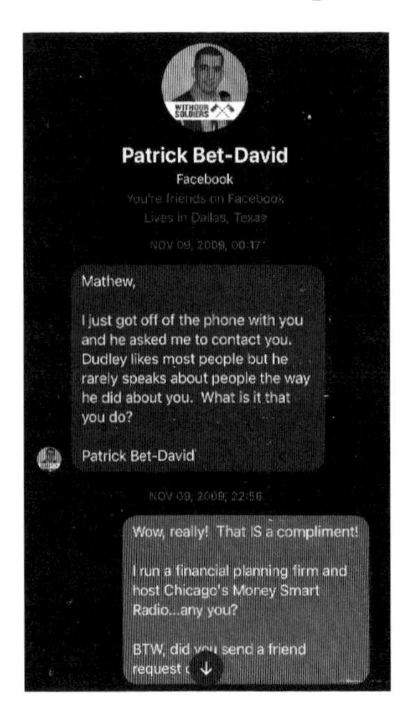

Unless you learn to read blessings as opportunities, you'll miss out on your miracle. The Bible contains examples of people who experienced financial miracles with both spiritual and material wealth as well.

I never thought I would be an entrepreneur in a million years or end up in the insurance industry. In fact, our company has over 20,000 agents, and 89% of them never had any insurance industry experience or previously had an insurance license. Yet, we find ourselves with an opportunity to financially change our lives by first helping others get closer to their goals and dreams. We find ourselves in one of the most noble and virtuous industries ever created.

The third servant did not take advantage of the opportunity he was given. I refused to miss out on opportunities because I am not open to trying something new.

THREE SIGNS TO UNCOVER IF YOU'RE BURYING YOUR TALENTS

If digging holes to hide your talent is something you're in the habit of doing, you need to stop now! Remember, it has nothing to do with the *number* of talents given but everything to do with what the person *did* with them after the master left town.

Sometimes burying talents, gifts, resources, influence, and power (and whatever God has given you) seems easier. Still, there is always a greater reward for doing something with what God has entrusted to you. Use your God-given talents! You owe it to yourself to live up to your potential. This needs to be shared with every generation. Everyone—including young people, need to realize they have talents. When they do, invest and watch out for the common pitfalls.

1. Comparison

Use the talents you've been given as best as possible and refuse to compare to others with different or more talents.

If you've buried your talent, why do you think you've been burying your talent? Maybe you've been suppressing it because you believe it's not as good as someone else's. Then, you look around and think you shouldn't do anything because it's so seemingly small.

People lack insight into what their talents actually are. As a result, they either think less of their abilities or too highly of what they can do. The more you develop skills and abilities in a specific area, the better you can assess and use your talents.

I looked at where I was compared to others when I started entrepreneurship. While I was using my talents, I was so far behind. Everyone around me was buying cars and houses and getting married, but I was struggling as a single dad. So I had to understand that I wasn't on the same track.

Some people's process is linear—especially those who aren't in business for themselves. For other people, their process is different. When I was funding my dream, it felt like I was pouring money into a bottomless pit. Yet, the more you invest in it, you'll eventually reach the bottom, and start climbing out to become profitable.

2. Doubting Abilities

If you are constantly focusing on your flaws, you may be doubting your abilities which will hinder you from putting your best foot forward.

- Are you your own worst critic? Most of us tend to be. I get it when you have to critique yourself because you want to improve yourself, but make sure it is positive.
- Are you hesitant to post something on social media? People will have something to say regardless of what you do or don't do. Don't hold back from being who you are to appease other people.
- Have you thought about starting a business or saving money? Most people have ideas they never follow through with

because they don't think it will work, or people may question them rather than support them—including spouses and close friends.

- What would people you love say if you invest in yourself? If you never mention it or ask them, you'll never know.

All of these things stem from fear which we discussed in chapter three. It has a subtle way of showing up—the servant who was given one talent operated out of fear. Your abilities will lead to opportunities. Opportunities will lead to actions that create results. Those results and the awareness to increase your skill set that will create confidence. Your confidence will deepen your faith. It's an endless cycle. So pray like it's up to God, but work like it's up to you.

I have been guilty of burying quite a few talents. In fact, you are looking at one right now. I wanted to write a book for over a decade, but I put it off. Then haphazardly, I put a rough draft together but didn't get it published.

During the recession in 2007, I was being pulled in every direction. I was in radio and television and didn't consider having someone help me. Instead of evoking teamwork, I thought of myself and what I could do. I was thinking about costs, coordination, patience, and time. I operated just like the third guy with his talent.

I never thought to use my faith due to thinking so small. I was reluctant whenever I went to an event, and someone asked if I had a book because I knew I needed to do it. I realized my lack of faith was hindering people from unburying their talents and operating in faith.

Since then, I've learned how to ask the right questions, allow God to direct my path, and trust that He will answer the questions along the way. I thought I couldn't do it because of my ignorance of the publishing and book industry, and writing is one of my weaknesses. So I stopped letting those insecurities hinder me from using the resources right in front of me.

Do you want to put a stop to that faulty logic to stop burying your talents? To be the kind of servant who puts yourself out there to double your talent, like the wise servants, you need to be willing to say, "This isn't about *me*; this is about me using what I've been given me to bring Him glory, to make Him known."

Your talents are not just for you. They were given to you so that you could serve others. Apostle Peter wrote, "Each of you should use whatever gift you have received to serve others, as faithful stewards of God's grace in its various forms" (1 Peter 4:10).

Look at what God has given you, and ask yourself how you're using your talents to serve others around you. If you can't come up with anything, you need to start doing something.

There is a warning at the end of the parable: "For whoever has will be given more, and they will have an abundance.

Whoever does not have, even what they have will be taken from them." What does that mean? Just like the servants in the Parable of the Talents—the one who did nothing had his talent taken and given to the one who had the most. Think about the message you are sharing when you bury your talents. Does it mean you are a lazy servant? Do you deserve to lose what you've been given and watch it be handed to someone else—since it was never yours in the first place? If you don't want to be seen that way, do something with your talents.

3. Disappointment

Maybe you've buried your talent because you've been burned by trying to use your gifts and talents before, and you don't want to feel that feeling ever again. I've been burned numerous times. As a matter of fact, one of the biggest reasons I buried the talent of writing a book is because it was going to be released before I had a chance to approve it. Instead of working with me, the company I signed with actually made me buy back the rights to my book so it wouldn't be published.

So I know all too well about trying to do something and it didn't go too well. Instead of trying again, you've decided to bury what God has given you out of disappointment. That same talent took a decade to unbury, but it's here now. And I encourage you dig up talents you've buried. Your future self will thank you.

People see the success and the views I get on social media now, but it hasn't always been that way. Most people have no idea how reluctant I was when I started recording YouTube videos. For years, I was not getting views. I uploaded video after video in hopes that I was making an impact. Unfortunately, I had no way to know because no one left any feedback.

When I left the jobs I was working to work full-time in my own company; I battled fear of failure and success. There have been many times I had marketing seminars, and no one showed up. So I learned to use those times to propel me to keep going.

It was discouraging, but I kept showing up. It wasn't until I did Vlogmas—a series of daily vlogs during Christmastime—in 2020, where I unpacked the Bible from the lens of an entrepreneur, that people even began to watch my videos. As a result of that one video, I unburied even more talents which included leadership, training, and how to provide opportunities. As a result, I hired a team and created jobs. It exploded our channel to over 100k subscribers and we earned a plaque from YouTube after crossing that milesone.

USE YOUR SKILLS TO SELL

2 Kings 4:1-7 tells the story of the widow with the oil. The husband left her without money, and her late husband's creditors promised to take her sons as slaves. Elisha asked her what she had so he could help. She responded that she had nothing—except a small jar of oil. Then Elisha gave her instructions.

The prophet commanded her to find every empty jar she could—even if it meant getting them from her neighbors. So she and her children listened to the prophet and got to work. When they received the empty jars, the prophet commanded her to pour oil into them. She had one jar of oil, but the oil would not stop flowing as she kept pouring it into other jars. She kept pouring and filled another jar.

The oil miraculously stopped when they filled the last jar. Most people think the story ends there, and the miracle is her having more than enough. But then the prophet told her to *go* and *sell the oil* to pay her debts, with one jar of oil equaling a yearly salary.

He commanded her to sell. People weren't just going to come to her house. She had to go to the marketplace, set up a table, and market it. She had to put herself out there and get others to sample it so they would potentially want to buy it.

The story doesn't specify how many jars she had or how much her debt was. However, some Scriptures confirm her household was taken care of for the rest of her life. She operated out of faith, not fear or logical understanding.

Let me also add that he told her to pay off her debt—with her income—because her husband probably never knew about life insurance or had an agent sit down with him to understand the importance of it. Okay, shameless plug for my industry. What do you expect? I told you we had to sell!

FOUR T'S TO TAP INTO YOUR TALENTS

Entrepreneurs are passionate, volatile, growth-hungry individuals. By definition, an entrepreneur is a person who organizes and operates a business (or businesses), taking on greater than normal financial risks in order to do so. We are willing to take risks and go against the grain of societal norms to escape the rat race, shed our inhibitions, and eagerly look forward to a future of exceptional success.

TENACITY

While our courageous disposition is compelling in pushing us to take the first step toward building a new future, it's not enough to keep us going when things get tough. The truth is that many people try to take on new risks without maximizing their current opportunities. When a new trend comes along, many abandon their current endeavors to pursue another shiny object.

With this mindset, we'll miss one of the most critical but overlooked entrepreneurial skills: tenacity. Instead of pivoting when sales or income has plateaued, some entrepreneurs put what they are working on in park and jump on the next thing moving—the new shiny toy; however, I'm addicted to mastery. I refuse to get distracted when something new comes along. Instead, I want to see things to completion.

The temptation to quit posting on YouTube and Instagram was real. Of course, I believed in what I was sharing but failed to see a return. However, I held on to what I believed. I worked more diligently, created a content strategy, and implemented it. I listened and valued my team's ideas about creating content about faith for Vlogmas, and it worked. One Vlogmas video alone reached over 520,000 people!

Just remember, it's not necessarily about what you do; it's about what you finish. Cultivate tenacity through consistent work and courage. If you wonder why you haven't been blessed from a financial standpoint—are you operating with tenacity?

Are you striving to improve your skillset instead of quitting when you are three feet from gold? I'm not talking about going to college and getting a degree—student loan debt is real. It can be anything from an internship to YouTube University. No one will knock on your door and ask if you want a job. But, if you refuse to add value or invest in your craft, you will see nothing in return. God didn't forget to bless you along the way, but when you fail to move with tenacity, you'll remain where you are.

One day, a college student sent me a DM on Instagram and offered his marketing services. Out of faith, he asked if he could take pictures and create some promotional material for me. I said yes, and he took two trains and a bus ride to get to my office, take photos of our workshop, and edit them for delivery via email the same evening. He ended up serving his way into a position and became a part of my team, working full-time. That's what I call tenacity. This brings me to my next point—your team.

TEAM

The successful people in your life are only one or two memories away from reliving what it's like to be broke. They are the same people who can sustain their wealth because they care about people. They understand the power of a team.

Being an awesome leader is the only way you can have an incredible team. If leading people is beneath you, leadership is not for you. It's about coaching, directing, elevating, and firing people, and doing it with humility and developing the excellence in others.

Surrender Pride

Pride gets no pleasure from having something, only out of having more than the next person. Comparison and thinking more highly of yourself makes you prideful: the pleasure of being above others. Proverbs 11:2 says, "When pride comes, then comes disgrace, but with humility comes wisdom."

As the world continues to evolve, I know I have to be open to learning from younger people as well as older people. Eight, ten, and fifteen-year-olds on YouTube are reviewing toys, comics, video games, and baseball cards. They make hundreds of thousand dollars a year before graduating junior high or high school.

Pride refuses to be taught or enlightened because it knows everything. Humility will look to see what someone is doing so adjustments can be made to improve.

The oldest person on my social media team is around twenty-two, *almost* half my age. However, these young men have been on social media since junior high. They have ten years of experience. As Malcom Gladwell writes in *Outliers,* "The key to mastering a skill is practice, and ten thousand hours is the magic number of greatness." I'd say they've had plenty of practice.

My team helped our YouTube channel grow from 5,000-10,000 subscribers to 183,000 subscribers because of their insight. They know how to create headlines and thumbnails that attract the current generation. With the help of a team, I've been able to teach, coach, and educate more people than I ever could have by myself while also allowing me to provide them with opportunities. Otherwise, these guys might just be bagging groceries and stocking shelves instead of doing something they're passionate about.

I have to learn new things because entrepreneurship and capitalism will humble you very quickly if you don't adjust. The marketplace will remind you that there's somebody just like you down the street, and if I'm not changing and adapting, I won't be able to impact as many people.

Your team does not have to be people you connect with and work with on a daily basis. You can partner with people for different projects—partner with others based on your weaknesses. If someone else does something better than you, let them do it. It's not a competition; it's collaboration.

My team gets to be around people like Patrick Bet-David, Kevin Hart, Tim Tebow, Tim Grover, David Goggins, Kurt Warner, Leila Ali, General "Mad Dog" Mattis, Deion Sanders, Shaq, Eric Thomas, and the late great Kobe Bryant. I want them to be exposed to greatness. I want them to elevate their identity.

Seek Mentorship

Mentors are a part of your team. Who is pouring into you? You have to be held accountable to a proven mentor. People used to think mentors were in short supply. They aren't. It is mentees that are a dime a dozen. The marketplace is looking for proven mentors out there.

Do you want to know how to quickly kill and buy into the fear of your financially free aspirations? Talk to broke people. Talk to people who don't have a big dream of their own and find joy in keeping you down at their level, so they don't have to do work themselves to keep up with you.

Many new inventions, game-changing businesses, and generation-shifting decisions are shot down before they even get a start by "bouncing your ideas" off someone with no faith (not religion) of their own. However, once people find their faith-made path to obtain wealth, most of them are open-minded to provide guidance for those seeking help.

The majority of millionaires I know who mentor people are kind-hearted people, contrary to my previous belief. Mentors don't have time to waste because they are working on the next goal or coming up with new ideas, which is why you have to find a reason for them to mentor and coach you.

If you have been approaching mentors on Instagram, commenting about the material things they have, and then asking if they will be your mentor—you probably won't get the response you want. Asking one or two times doesn't always result in the outcome you are looking for either. You could invest in their course, ministry, or mastermind group. If they have other products and services—like a book or conference—purchase their book and get a ticket to their event.

I remember telling my mentor, Patrick Bet-David, I was willing to do whatever I needed to do to win. I said, "Patrick, now that I'm forty-two, I want to let you know something. You can coach, teach, and tell me what I need to hear and what I need to know because I don't have any time to waste."

He looked back at me and said, "Are you sure? I'm not afraid to coach talent. What you need are systems and processes."

Since then, my wife and I have adopted a mindset called the speed of implementation. We don't have to be reminded three or four times when given ideas or instructions to improve certain areas. I am aware of how valuable time is, and I won't rest knowing there are things I can do to improve. I want to show our mentor we can obtain guidance once, implement it, and have the eagerness to show him results. The numbers speak for themselves. We have earned close to ten million dollars in under seven years under Patrick Bet-David's mentorship.

I didn't care about my feelings being hurt and if my ego was damaged. Some of the greatest advice I can give anyone ready for growth is:

1. Put ego aside.
2. Have humility.
3. Take notes.
4. Implement what you learn.

You can never go into situations thinking you know everything. So don't get too high on your highs or too low on your lows. Don't over-celebrate victories or over-mourn your losses.

Mentors motivate, inspire, and give direction. They give mentees the tools they need to achieve their goals and work through challenges; however, they don't necessarily have to be someone you are connected with personally.

A mentor should be someone who:

- Offers encouragement.
- Provides personal development tips.
- Shares knowledge and life experiences.
- Discusses goal-setting and aspirations.
- Advises professional development.
- Provides resources.
- Keeps you accountable.

Finding people who have been down the same road before will prevent you from making many mistakes. Connect with someone who knows how to create systems and processes and who has already figured this out and learn what fundamentals you need.

Surround Yourself with Successful People

Your success depends heavily on who you associate with. Your level of talent and potential is irrelevant if you're surrounded by people who don't help you see it. Most people adapt to whatever environment they find themselves in. Stop refusing to get around successful people because you don't find yourself on their level.

You'll repel successful people if you complain more than you take responsibility. This is because successful people take responsibility and ownership for *everything* in their life.

One of the most convincing messages of today is a victimhood and entitlement mentality. Today, the voice of the complainers has gotten bolder and louder, drowning out the message of those who implement a faith-made mindset that has conquered their setbacks, dire circumstances, and seeming lack of resources.

In his best-selling book, *Miracle Morning*, Hal Elrod wrote, "The moment you accept total responsibility for everything in your life is the day you claim the power to change anything in your life."

If you keep complaining about things you can't control, it's like broadcasting over a megaphone: "I want things to be *given* to me, and I won't stop complaining until that happens!" It shows you don't take control of the things you can control—your attitude, income, mindset, and behaviors and actions. Being helpless and excuse prone is a very noticable and unattractive quality.

Soak Up Knowledge

We have the world's information at our fingertips, so we must saturate ourselves with it from people on social media, YouTube, and those we interact with in person.

Exposing ourselves to new information fails if it stops right there. You must absorb that knowledge and implement it into your life. There was a brief time I worked as a YMCA lifeguard from 5-8 am. I would strategically take books and read while I was there. It was a time to soak in as much knowledge as I could. There was hardly anyone ever swimming at that time of the day. Remember *and* use the information you learn to become more successful and productive.

Let's say you attend a workshop or conference of like-minded thinkers. Maybe you take notes or discuss it over lunch with someone headed in the same direction as you. That's knowledge gained. As a result of the information, you're aware of something you didn't know before you attended, and now it's time for you to do something about it.

Now, fast forward a month. Can you remember the tips and tricks you learned? Are you actively applying them to your daily workflow to increase productivity? If the answer is no, you may have initially gained the knowledge—but you still must implement it for any wisdom to be achieved.

Share What You Know

We are in the era of hashtags, likes, and shares. People share memes, videos, business opportunities, and everything under the sun on social media. In this era, sharing knowledge and information with others is vital. People are already sharing; why not share something that will be helpful?

Sharing knowledge and inspiration fosters vision in others and strengthens relationships. It helps deepen your knowledge and engrains what you know. New conversations and opportunities can arise just from that gesture, offering even more opportunities to grow.

Success isn't just about what you accomplish in your life. It's about what you inspire others to do. After all, the teacher learns more than the student; teaching something as soon as you learn it is invaluable.

Sharpen Your Saw

A logger cut down fourteen trees on the first day. During the next few days, his production declined. He went from fourteen to ten, then nine. By the fourth day, he was only cutting down seven trees—half of what he originally cut. He couldn't get back to cutting down the number of trees he cut down on the first day despite his continued good efforts and ability.

Puzzled by his disappointing results, he asked for advice from someone he respected. The person told him, "Sharpen your saw." That advice changed everything for the logger once he realized what he had to do. It is essentially what Abraham

Lincoln said, "If I only had an hour to chop down a tree, I would spend the first forty-five minutes sharpening my axe."

Learn how to do things better. Focus on the client and their needs, and ensure you are delivering the best possible service to satisfy those needs.

Sometimes you need time away from your business to come back with a fresh perspective. An entrepreneur or person who desires to improve their life can also do this. Take time to step back from what you are doing with your personal finances and look for ways to make improvements. Remember, you can always ask for advice from an expert.

What is the most pressing issue for me to accomplish during the next quarter, half year, and the entire year? What skills do I need to achieve that goal, and how can I better increase my knowledge? What do I need to do to sharpen my saw?

With that said, how are you using your time? Assess what you are prioritizing by answering the following questions:

1. What's on my phone right now?
2. Are the apps I look at dozens of times a day serving to condition my spirit for creating wealth?
3. Who do I talk to the most?
4. Are the people I'm associated with at a place in life that I aspire to be?
5. How am I being pushed to the next level right now?

TWEAK THE SYSTEM

After meeting with Patrick after my event we implemented a new system. We created six steps. Within those steps, we had sub-steps and leadership development. As a result, we made $100k in nine months. From nine to fourteen months, we crossed $250k.

At months fourteen to seventeen, we shot up to $750k. By thirty-seven months, my wife and I became cash-flow millionaires, and we haven't looked back.

This was all made possible by Patrick's mentorship and my willingness to push aside my ego. We implemented everything Patrick told us to do. Since then, our impact and influence grew because we kept moving when momentum was on our side.

Once you think you have some form of financial freedom, the muscle that got you there won't be the muscle that keeps you there. So you'll have to keep working the muscle because it will require you to keep improving to maintain and increase your wealth.

Financial freedom requires you to improve, stay consistent, and make the right choices. If you've ever tried to improve your credit score, it starts increasing, then the next thing you know, you lost momentum and get behind one month. Boom—it drastically declines. Your credit drops fifty points and the bill takes a few years to drop off your credit report. It's the same way with achieving financial freedom. You can't afford to get behind!

TRUST AND EMBRACE THE PROCESS

"The Process" is a series of steps someone must take to achieve the desired result. Some steps can be toilsome, take a long time, and seem pointless or painful. This universal process reminds me of one of the greatest basketball players of all time. Not only did he trust the process when it came to basketball, but he also embraced the process of becoming an entrepreneur.

Michael Jordan has often rehashed the popular legend that he was cut from the Laney High School varsity basketball team as a sophomore, inspiring him to work harder and get better.

All basketball hopefuls tried out for Coach Herring in the fall of 1978. Coach Herring assigned Jordan, along with the other promising underclassmen, to the junior varsity team, with the exception of his friend, classmate, and rival, Leroy Smith. However, Jordan's hard work and fortuitous growth spurt turned him from a gangly teenager into the Laney varsity alpha dog his senior year.

We held a leadership retreat at the Breakers Hotel in Palm Beach and watched the Netflix special on Michael Jordan called *The Last Dance.* Air Jordan is a legend because of his incredible ability to gain lightning-fast position on his opponents, leap high, and span seemingly inhuman amounts of air to the basket. However, few people realize that Michael spent five years as a pro-basketball player before he and his team earned their first championship in 1991.

Jordan was consistently hitting between thirty and forty points each game, but he was equally getting pounded in the paint by much stronger opponents. This was especially true of the Bull's arch rivals, the Detroit Pistons, and Boston Celtics. As a result, Jordan started training with Tim Grover.

Jordan eventually became the number one scorer on his team. It was all about Mike. Everyone knew to pass the ball to him for them to win. However, it was short-lived because he realized he had to build up people around him and work together as a team.

Jordan's coach, Phil Jackson, took the ball out of Mike's hand. Thus, Mike learned leadership skills of pushing and guiding his teammates instead of being the focal point of every game. Scottie Pippen and other Bulls players were given the opportunity to be recognized for their abilities (talents) as well.

The Chicago Bulls went on to win three straight championships from 1991 to 1993 and another three consecutive titles from 1996 to 1998. Six rings later, Michael Jordan is on top of the world, known simply as one of the greatest ever to play the game. Not only did he have championships to show for his efforts, he learned about delayed gratification, which is one of the most vital attributes of being in leadership and entrepreneurship.

Michael turned his own last name into a synonym for greatness. His iconic sneaker brand became one of the most profitable shoe lines in the world. Across some four decades, Jordan has earned $1.7 billion (pre-tax) off the court from brands such as Nike, Coca-Cola, McDonald's, Wheaties, and Chevrolet, to name a few. Jordan still maintains official ties with Nike, Hanes, Gatorade, and Upper Deck.[4]

He recognized that his greatest endorsement was what he did on the court because if it were not for those efforts, he would not have partnerships with other name brands.

No matter what adversity came his way, Michael Jordan believed in his talents, used them when no one else believed in them, and refused to compromise his career.

Everyone has a bankable talent. You came to earth for a purpose. On the deepest level, you are here for a spiritual purpose—to discover your identity and value. You also have a form of expression in the world, to serve others while fulfilling yourself. Do not stop until you have tapped into your talent and expressed it. It is why you are here.

When doing anything unfamiliar, it is expected that you will feel doubt and discomfort. It's normal to wonder, "What if this doesn't work?" especially with our time being so precious and we already feel overwhelmed by all we need to accomplish. When other people were creating YouTube videos and they didn't get a lot of traction in the beginning either, including

[4]Paul Rudder, How much money does Michael Jordan earn? Salary, net worth and endorsements, February 2022

my mentor, it was reassurance that it was all a part of the process.

Trusting the process means staying committed even when it looks like it's not working, worth it, or if you're arriving at the desired destination. Enjoy the process. I'm not talking about going to the park for a Sunday picnic, but if I start to feel overwhelmed, I remind myself that there's a purpose in this process, and I trust that God is taking care of things I can't see. I have to remind myself even when the purpose is not evident. I notice it, acknowledge it, and decide to act in faith anyway. That's trust.

Although I want to know everything God is doing, I've learned that finding information along the way can be as enjoyable as I allow it to be. I tell myself it's okay if I'm ignorant of the future or if I lack some of the pieces to the puzzle. The process doesn't change, but my perception does. My attitude and discipline change me, and it starts to feel different because I think differently about it.

Believe it or not, most people get rich because they find a way to earn it using their God-given talents, not because of an incredible stroke of luck. Instead, they figure out what it takes to make a lot of money, take action, thus creating the conditions for even more wealth.Take stock of your talents. What comes easily and naturally to you? What would you do even if you weren't getting paid for it? What compliments do you receive from others? These are all clues to discover your talent. Instead of burying them, multiply what you've been given.

6

Broke Isn't Biblical

"Remember this—you can't serve God and money, but you can serve God with money."
— **Selwyn Hughes**

My kids and I were getting ready for church in the middle of a Chicago winter. Before we headed out, I stopped them one by one to check if they put their shoes on the right feet. As soon as we stepped outside, the frigid Chicago wind and snow flurries swirled around us. I corralled the kids to hurry so we didn't miss the train.

I was broke. My debit card had a negative balance with overdraft fees, and I maxed out my credit cards. The dealership had repossessed my car. Despite everything crashing over me, I refused to let my circumstances deter me from keeping my faith. I knew going to church would give me the encouragement I needed to carry on.

Thankfully, we stepped on the train with ease, but when we arrived at our stop downtown, the church was still almost a mile away. I reached in my pocket, pulled out my wallet, and opened it to see if I had a few dollars for a cab or bus, but I had nothing.

I grabbed my children's hands, and we began to walk. A few minutes later, my daughter, about seven at the time, broke the silence and our pace and said, "Papi, I'm cold. I'm hungry."

Frustration crept in. "Why didn't you get your gloves? Why didn't you eat?" I retorted.

Before she could respond, I immediately wanted to take back what I had just said. It wasn't her fault. It was mine because I'm the parent. So why was I taking my anger out on her? I should be mad at myself because if I had paid the car note, we wouldn't be walking to church cold and hungry.

Immediately, I said, "I'm sorry, babe. I shouldn't have been ugly to you."

I skimmed the nearest place to get out of the cold weather. Jimmy John's was across the street. We felt a gust of warm air when we walked into the restaurant.

The cashier smiled from behind the register and said, "Hello, can I take your order?"

"Oh, we just stopped in to warm up," I replied with an uneasy smile.

"But Papi, I'm hungry," my daughter pleaded, gently pulling on my arm.

There were a few seconds of awkward silence as I looked at my kids and the cashier. *What do I do?* I looked at the menu to buy time because I knew my debit card would decline the moment I slid it into the machine.

I calculated the cheapest thing on the menu to feed my kids. Eight dollars. All I needed was eight dollars—plus tax. The only thing I could think to use was my secured credit card because I didn't have an unlimited or a high-limit card at that time.

Looking at the cashier, I placed the order. Then, I silently prayed, "Lord, you promised me that the birds don't have to worry about what they would eat. You said in your Word everything in your creation does not have to worry and fear. So today, I do not fear sliding this credit card because, by faith, some credit will be there."

I sealed my prayer in Jesus' name and handed my credit card to the cashier. I admit I had an ounce of skepticism but fed my faith instead of my fear. I held my breath and paused to see if it would go through.

Instead of telling me it declined, she handed my card back to me and said, "Your order will be ready in a moment, sir."

God performed a miracle that day. When the kids and I sat down, all I could say was, "God is good. God is awesome."

I split the sandwich in half like communion bread and placed it in front of them. They ate their chips and sandwich and finished it off with a drink. I ate one bite and a few of the chip crumbs they had left.

I will never forget experiencing God's grace that day. I know I didn't deserve it, yet God allowed me to feed my family. The same way my daughter told me she was hungry was the same way I went to my Heavenly Father and told Him I needed Him. While it was not God's fault that I didn't have resources, He made sure to supply my needs. I was in a place of desperation, and God showed up.

WHAT GOD SAYS ABOUT MONEY

Jesus used illustrations of money in His parables. He called out those hoarding their money and called the rich Pharisees sinners and hypocrites. In the Bible, we read stories from Joseph in Egypt to Lydia of Thyatira, and we discern wealth is a blessing and a responsibility we're meant to steward well. Jesus said, "I have come that you might have life, and have it more abundantly" (John 10:10). He wants you to fulfill your God-given purpose, to walk out the dreams He's placed in your heart.

The Bible teaches us how God is the giver of all riches. It's not solely a person's own doing. It also says that God can take away riches as quickly as He gives them, so we shouldn't set our hearts and minds on money. Whatever money we have, we can use it to further the kingdom.

Today, many overly devout religious people focus only on what happens after they leave the earth. But God also wants to affect your life right now, today. My daughter wasn't focused on how much I loved Jesus when her stomach was growling. She *needed* food. And I *needed* money to buy food.

Our relationship with money is directly tied to our behavior. Currently, your mindset on money influences your financial decisions, and those actions lead to your results. For example, suppose you feel like money is running your life, you're struggling to generate more income, or if you feel overwhelmed with finances, you're more likely to spend irresponsibly.

First you, must discover the lies you believe about money because it will fuel a wrong mindset. Once you discover and destroy the lies, you will begin to heal your relationship with money and have it empower you rather than overwhelm you.

God desires you to have a good relationship with money. However, suppose you are just beginning your entrepreneurship journey. In that case, you may fall into two camps regarding your relationship with money: The "I have to spend money to make money" camp or the "I'm afraid of spending and losing what I have" camp. Unfortunately, neither are comfortable places to be. They are common setbacks and can limit the growth of your business, and significantly impact your wealth and family.

In today's church world, two dominant financial theologies (gospels) stand in contrast to one another. Most churches live in either camp and govern their finances according to the tenets of the theology. To understand financial stewardship, we must examine these two gospels: the Poverty and the Prosperity Gospel. After we identify them, I will dive into the Word of God and show you what God's heart is concerning these matters and where we should apply our faith where money is concerned.

The Poverty Gospel

The church's earliest history and standard of living were what we consider poor today. The poverty mindset deems prosperity as non-materialistic. It also tends to consider possessions to be a curse. They nonchalantly believe God will provide for their basic needs as He does for the birds of the air.

Poverty avoids planning for the future because their daily needs preoccupy them too much. Their ability to help the poor is non-existent because they are the poor. Instead, they rely on Sriptures that tell the rich to sell or give all that they have to contribute to the poor (Luke 12:33).

For years I have heard people quote Matthew 26:11, "The poor will be with you always," as a way for people to blame the poor for their poverty, to justify inaction in the face of growing poverty and misery, and to claim that if God wanted to end poverty, He would do so.

Jesus doesn't condone poverty; He reminds us that God hates poverty and has commanded us to end poverty by paying our debts, using our talents to increase our income, and using wisdom to create wealth. The Scripture is often misused because it served as a reminder to the disciples that charity and hypocrisy will not end poverty.

Some Christians and religious leaders have a distorted view of money. Historically, that has been the case with much of the church. As a result, poverty has been glorified, and many Christians believe that success and ambition are evil. However, poverty is not glorified. Instead, the Bible refers to poverty (whether spiritual, emotional, relational, or financial) as a curse (Proverbs 18:22).

The Prosperity Gospel

You have heard of this before for some famous ministries promote this type of thinking. For example, the Prosperity Gospel, known as "Name-it and Claim-it," promises unlimited levels of material abundance.

You can find different styles of the prosperity gospel, but this prosperity gospel has only risen in the last thirty to forty years. An obsession with having material things can easily take control of our lives, and it saddens my heart. People will worship their cell phones, the latest fashions, and designer handbags instead of relying on their faith. Gadgets and clothing styles are often obsolete within days or weeks of purchase, but our faith is eternal.

Some of the most talented singers began in their church choir but left their faith to pursue fame and money. Then, they start praising not only money but also themselves. There's nothing wrong with pursuing a high-profile career or being proud of your success. Still, the problem lies when we seek sporting, academic, or artistic achievements to bring ourselves glory instead of realizing those things are temporary.

It's always a matter of the heart—which doesn't necessarily negate prosperity. You can put things before your faith in poverty too.

Another problem arises when we think that the evidence of obedience is prosperity. Now, wait a minute. Let me repeat that because this is a subtle shift in thinking. Scripture teaches that God frequently rewards obedience with material abundance. The problem arises when we think the evidence of our obedience and the proof of our righteousness is our prosperity.

Where in the Bible does it say that? When we think to ourselves, "Okay, I have a lot of material possessions in my life, so I am standing righteous before God. I have a substantial bank account, so God must be happy with me. The bigger my home, the newer my home, then the better I feel." This is not godliness because our righteousness comes from God and not from anything we do. It is a trick of the enemy to get us to take our eyes off God. The prosperity gospel is a ploy of the god of this age (2 Corinthians 4:4), and for the most part, American Christianity is wrapped up in this affluence.

Many people have been caught in this trap. Now, people may prosper because God is blessing them. However, no one can rely on financial prosperity or the blessings in their lives—the evidence of what they see as evidence of God's happiness with them. They could just be utilizing the laws I've discussed previously, which will yield a return. Plenty of people prosper who have nothing to do with God.

Please do not rely on your material abundance as a sign of obedience. If you do this, you are setting yourself up to be deceived by the god of this world.

On the flip side, we can't treat poverty and suffering as a sign of disobedience—although some consequences caused by irresponsibility can result in lack. The important thing is to learn from those choices. Many people have suffered and struggled with money and being able to pay their bills, and they are under condemnation, guilt, and shame. They think their lack of abundance is because God is not happy with them. God doesn't love them any less, and He can be pleased with them; however, they haven't accessed God's promises because they aren't applying the principles in the Good Book.

Both the poverty and prosperity gospels are in error. They are doctrinally unsound and unbalanced. It results in division and confusion—the opposite of what Christianity represents.

Stewardship

God's heart is to provide us with encouragement, resources, and instructions for financial gain, and He demonstrates to us what our relationship to material possessions is supposed to be. God's nature does not require poverty or prosperity but reliance on Him.

There's a difference between thinking that you own your money and knowing God owns your money. It is easy to get attached to thinking money is yours because every time you look at your bank account, property's title deed, and the receipt of your latest purchase, you see your name written on it. It tells you that the property belongs to you!

After all, you have worked hard for the things you have right now. Therefore, it is only right to believe that they truly belong to you. However, thinking that you, and you alone, have the right to your possession leads to a deadly trap of pride, greed, and selfishness.

The truth is that we don't own anything; we don't even own our life. It is God who gave it to us. Psalm 24:1 says, "The earth is the Lord's, and all its fullness, the world and those who dwell therein." If we believe this verse with all our hearts, it would be easier for us to share our blessings with other people. When you believe you are just the caretaker of your house, car, smartphone, laptop, computer, electronic gadgets, money, and others will cause you to have a healthy attachment to them.

Therefore, stewardship expresses our obedience regarding the administration of everything God has placed under our control, which is all-encompassing. Stewardship is the commitment of one's self and possessions to God's service, recognizing that we do not have the right of control over our property or ourselves.

GENERATIONAL POVERTY

When the Israelites came into the land of Canaan, God told them, "You will each have your own land." The land was given to them in proportion to the size of their family. He did not guarantee them equality of income or distribution. He guaranteed them equality of opportunity.

That is why some people in the Bible have, and some do not. If one man was lazy and did not work his land very much, he failed to receive abundance. Another man who toiled, tilled the land, and built homes was rewarded for his labor. People quickly realized that they were in partnership with God.

Therefore, if we took all the world's wealth and redistributed it evenly amongst all men and women, within one year, it would be back in the hands of those who had it previously. That is because the majority of people never learned how to steward money. The minority who knew how to control it and understood the principle of investment and return would have received their money back.

God knew that it would not take long for a minority to get the land back from the people who were given an equal share. That is why every fifty years, it was like, "Sorry, guess what? The monopoly game is over. We are shaking up the board and will return everything to the original ancestral families."

God knew the greed in most men's hearts to accumulate for themselves at the expense of all the others, so He put this mechanism in place to keep everything on a level playing field.

The principle is that God wants every family to have resources to produce their livelihood. This was the mechanism for correcting any errors. If the land did not come back to someone during their lifetime, it could return to their children.

POOR VS. BROKE

A broke mentality develops through years of mental and circumstantial conditioning that tells people to believe they never have enough money. Or, when they do have money, they make poor financial decisions driven by fear or the need for instant gratification.

How many people do you know have been broke? Shoot, I've been broke, but there's a big difference between being broke and being poor.

Broke is a temporary situation. When I filed for bankruptcy, I was flat-out broke. I was making more credit card payments than I was earning income. I'd make bi-weekly paycheck advances just to keep up. When I didn't have enough money for food to feed my kids as a single dad, I was broke. When bill collectors blew up my phone, and I would never answer, I was broke. When I lowered my head in shame every time I saw people who loaned me money, I was broke.

However, being poor is a condition of the spirit and character. Sadly, parents can unconsciously pass this down to their children. Many go through life with a poor spirit hanging over them and have no idea.

LIFE CHANGING ADVICE FROM FAITH BASED MILLIONAIRES

So, what's the difference between being broke and being poor? Being broke is a temporary scenario you can eventually get out of, but being poor means, you've given up on life and feel helpless. Staying poor is a choice! When I was broke, I refused to have a poverty, victim, or entitlement mindset, which eventually helped me rise. Before you read any further, take a moment and listen to some life-changing advice from faith-made millionaires.

HANDLE DEBT GOD'S WAY

Many Scriptures give us direction and instruction about how to handle money, specifically debt. Let me start by saying that I have been in situations where I had no choice but to use debt (a credit card, personal loan, etc.) to pay for emergencies—and it made me feel awful.

The truth is debt is equal to slavery. Proverbs 22:7 says, "The rich rule over the poor, and the borrower is a slave to the lender." So when you are in debt, you are entrapped—a captive, chained, and in service to the lender that issued the loan.

I remember a family member loaning me a rent payment when I was broke. I felt guilty, ashamed, anxious, and physically ill over that loan until it was paid in full.

Until you are debt-free, you will be enslaved to your past mistakes. You can move forward in God's grace, but the consequences of your actions will follow you until the debts are paid in full.

I find it interesting that many parallels between salvation and financial terminology in the Bible are made. For example:

- "The wages of sin is death" (Romans 6:23).
- "And because of Him, you are in Christ Jesus, who became to us wisdom from God, righteousness and sanctification and redemption" (1 Corinthians 1:30).
- "In Him, we have redemption through his blood, the forgiveness of our trespasses, according to the riches of His grace" (Ephesians 1:7).

Faith gives us hope and a future. Debt, in many cases, is a poor financial choice and keeps us from living out our God-given purpose. We should not be enslaved to anything or anyone, including financial decisions.

Suppose you saw my kids and me when we were walking in the cold, and they had worry written all over their faces. If you asked them, "What's wrong?" And they responded, "We're not sure whether our dad is going to feed us," you would question my parenting, maybe even the love I had for my kids. Yet so many of the Lord's children do this. They live as if their Father in Heaven either isn't concerned or able to take care of their needs which is not true.

Our primary focus must be, "Lord, help me to use what You have given me to further Your kingdom." Your bank account is a reflection of your awareness, your savings is a reflection of your habits, and your credit score is a reflection of your attitude.

I fell into more than $20k of debt as soon as I came back from my first deployment because I rushed into a marrage that never should have happened. Out of panic and desperation, I called a bankruptcy lawyer to file for bankruptcy. I had no idea what it even was at the time. The amount of money I owed became too much to bear. I just wanted a way to get out from under it.

Perhaps you aren't in debt because of an emergency, but because of your own spending habits, living above your means, or just careless budgeting and overspending (been there, done that, got out of it, and so can you). Again, you aren't alone. The greatest part is that you can show yourself grace and move forward because now you know better!

Psalm 37:21 says, "The wicked borrow and do not repay, but the righteous give generously." I remember when I paid off debt on a low income while struggling to pay mortgage and water bills each month.

No one forced me to spend money I did not have. I had a load of debt and no income to pay it off. Repaying our debts honors God and is the morally right thing to do.

God will not hate you or shun you if you have debt; however, I believe that unless we attempt all that we can to pay what we owe, we are not honoring God with our finances and cannot receive the full blessing from God.

We Cannot Serve God and Money

No one can serve two masters. Either you will hate one and love the other, or you will be devoted to the one and despise the other. Therefore, you cannot serve both God and money (Matthew 6:24).

I genuinely feel when I was debt-ridden, frustrated, and stressed about money, I was serving money. Think about it. When you don't know how you'll pay next month's electric bill, money becomes everything to you. When you're in debt, it consumes your life. You think about it when you eat dinner, when you're about to sleep, and when you wake up.

God wants to teach us how to handle our money wisely so that it doesn't have to consume so much of our time, energy, and thoughts. Value-aligned spending does not just apply to our finances. It applies to our lives holistically, so it's much easier to serve God than money when we live below our means, debt-free, and give because it's one less thing we have to worry about in our already busy lives.

I talk about money for a living, and yes, I have financial goals, but over time, I've developed habits and discipline that help me not think about money every single day, including debt freedom.

Leave Worry at the Door

Worrying never changes reality. The Good Book says that worrying won't add any years to your life. In fact, worry may even shorten your years due to the harmful effects on your health.

It's good to think about things we can do to change but consuming our thoughts with fixed matters is futile. In either case, worry produces nothing and contradicts having faith in something greater than yourself and your current circumstances.

Jesus, in the New Testament of the Bible, made the rebuke, "O you of little faith,"—he is talking about the heart of worry (Matthew 8:26). I believe all worry stems from our lack of faith in God.

We who have trusted God with our eternal destiny can easily fall into unbelief regarding the immediate problems we face, especially basic provisions. Even believers or people you think are religious can find themselves without faith.

Money Is *Not* the Root of All Evil

People say that money is the root of all evil. But if you ask them why they respond, "Because the Bible said so." However, is this what the Bible says? Let's read 1 Timothy 6:10: "For the *love of money* is the root of all evil: while some coveted after, they have erred from the faith, and pierced themselves through with many sorrows" (emphasis added).

The love of money is the beginning of every bad thing that occurs in this world. If you desire riches so much that you are willing to give up your salvation, you are committing the fatal mistake of loving money. In Matthew 16:26, Christ asks us, "For what profit is it to a man if he gains the whole world, and loses his own soul?"

As a result of loving money, what happens? People have "erred from the faith and have pierced themselves through with many sorrows." History is marred by endless examples of people who have lost everything simply because they love their money more than their spouse, children, family, friends, reputation, character, and above all, faith.

Some people can't get enough of it. When they reach a certain income level, they become discontent and find more ways to spend money. Of course, there's nothing wrong with improving yourself and your living condition, but learn to be grateful for what you have even while you go after your dreams.

To avoid discontentment and an insatiable hunger for more wealth, we must look at money the way God looks at money. We must know how to handle and view money from a faith-based perspective. Why? Because it will ultimately lead to greater blessings that are not just physical but also spiritual.

Don't commit the mistake of loving money; it's not worth it. It is a road that you don't want to tread. While it is *not* a sin to be rich, loving money is.

The Bible urges Christians to use whatever riches they have to bless others and glorify God. If Heaven has streets made with gold, why would He have a problem with someone buying a Rolex? Why would He have a problem with someone wearing red bottoms? If you aren't creating your identity and status around your finances, God doesn't have a problem with you having something. You can have money and still love God.

God Enables You to Acquire Wealth

The moment we don't acknowledge the true Source of our blessings is when we become poor. All good things come from God, and we have missed the point if we ascribe the glory to ourselves.

Deuteronomy 8:18 tells us, "And you shall remember the Lord your God, *for it is He who gives you power to get wealth*, that He may establish His covenant which He swore to your fathers, as it is this day" (emphasis added). Did you catch that? God gives us life and strength and improve our financial condition. He grants us wisdom and intellect—which we will discuss in chapter seven. If it weren't for God, we wouldn't be able to provide food, clothing, or shelter for our families. He gives us the power to get wealth; we must never forget that.

Money Is Needed to Do Good Works

Why do you want to be rich? It will all come to nothing if you have the wrong motives. Do you know that the Bible reveals why God blesses us with wealth?

2 Corinthians 9:8 says, "And God is able to make all grace abound toward you, that you, always having all sufficiency in all things, may have an abundance for every good work."

There's the reason, my friend! God blesses us so that we can bless others. So if the main reason we acquire wealth is to be a fountain of blessings to others, God will undoubtedly bless us according to His bounty and purpose.

Ministry isn't free, but the impact that you can make is priceless. During one of my times serving in ministry, my children and I went to feed the homeless. Instead of just going to tell people about Jesus we stopped by a restaurant. I ordered fifty meals of chicken and rice to take to them; so not only did we bless the homeless, we blessed a local business to prepare the meals.

So not only would I be able to tell people about how good God is, but I could also show them. My children sang to them and told them that God loved them, and we all worshipped together.

CIRCULATION OF MONEY

Smaug, the dragon in *The Hobbit*, hoarded up a vast pile of wealth, and then he just hung out in his cave, sitting on it. Over the last forty years, this is what some people think rich people do. However, this is not an accurate depiction of how wealthy people steward their resources.

Rabbi Daniel Lapin, known as America's Rabbi and a noted rabbinic scholar, best-selling author of *Thou Shalt Prosper*, says, "The sooner we get away from bills, the sooner we can start contributing." For example, paying someone to mow your lawn may make more sense instead of spending Saturdays doing yard work. You could be working on your business instead of trimming bushes or raking leaves.

The Jewish culture believes in circulating money so they can create generational wealth and focus on other valuable things.

Unbeknownst to me, I did this when I hired multiple sitters and nannies to pick my kids up and care for them when I worked.

In the Jewish tradition, there is nothing wrong with being wealthy. For Jews, the spiritual and ethical issues surrounding money focus on how one acquires wealth and what one does with it, and not with wealth itself. Just like any other material blessing, financial well-being has no intrinsic value. How we *use* it determines its value and measures our character.

GIFT OF GIVING

I've heard people say, "If I give to God, God will give to me. If I do not give, I do not have a right to go to God and have Him take care of my needs." While God honors what we give, this does not accurately illustrate giving.

Giving a tenth of your income, or tithing, existed before the Law of Moses. Abraham tithed to Melchizedek (Genesis 14:20; Hebrews 7:6), and Jacob vowed to tithe to the Lord at Bethel (Genesis 28:22). This practice was later codified in the law. Therefore, tithing is a biblical practice that precedes the law. However, the principle of tithing is a part of the heritage of all Abraham's descendants.

We are not required to give; however, we recognize that it is a principle that benefits us. In a sense, you could say, "We are under the law of tithing," if by "law" you meant a principle—as in the way you would say, "the law of gravity" or "the law of supply and demand."

God established giving to establish order in our finances, support the church, and prosper us. Of course, we do not have to give or tithe, but aligning our finances with biblical principles will keep us grounded.

The money and blessings you give come back manifold and overflowing. Call it tithing, charity, or karma according to your own faith, but it is a fact of how money works. Being generous begets generosity (Proverbs 22:9).

All faiths try to give guidance on issues of wealth inequality in society. Many Jews believe that as members of God's family, they have to look after each other—the same way God was looking after my children and me after leaving Jimmy John's.

I was extremely relieved when my kids and I finally made it to church. I didn't realize it then, but I was exercising my faith. After I worshipped God and emptied myself of all my worries and anxieties, I went the rest of the day without eating. I kept my heart on how good God was no matter what mental turmoil tried to come my way.

Times were tough, but I relied on my faith and learned how to get out of debt. I reminded myself to remember God when times were good. In the darkest moments, leaning on faith is the fabric of every great entrepreneur, athlete, and leader. That faith is fueled when it is connected to an awareness that you are serving something greater than yourself.

Giving doesn't just happen in church or ministry. I've been in a position where I could barely do for my kids, so I always look for ways to give back.

There was a time I went shopping at Men's Warehouse. I was browsing and I overheard a converstion between a mother and her son.

He brought her a pair of shoes he wanted her to buy. She held the box and slightly turning it. Looking away, she handed them back to him. "No, Papi, put that back. It's too expensive. We already have too much." she explained.

Immediately his disposition changed. His shoulders slightly dropped, but he obliged.

After watching them for a few more minutes, I headed to the register.

I leaned over the counter, "Excuse me, please put whatever that mother and son are buying on my credit card. I'll continue to shop. Don't tell them it was me. Just tell them God loves them."

I made sure I was out of their view when they finished shopping. Then, after I saw them exit the store, I went back up to the register, got my credit card, and went home.

I do that as often as I'm led because I know people who are in need. I want to help as many people as I can. I've had the same exact look as that mother did. I have felt what she felt. I've had to tell my children countless times to put something back because I wasn't able to get it for them.

That's why I love what I do today—because every day, I relate, speak, and encounter people who are in a similar predicament I was in. I've had moments of brokenness and moments of shame. I've had times when I questioned who I was and felt discouraged as a provider because I couldn't even feed my own kids.

God had been trying to get my attention for so long, and when he finally had it, I didn't look back. Realizing being broke isn't biblical gave me the freedom to have faith and wealth.

My past and present mistakes taught me some of the greatest life lessons that have transformed me. My faith reminded me that if I experienced a situation, I would get through it. God trusted me to invoke more faith into becoming a bigger blessing to others.

You can be as rich as the problems you solve and the value you create. Once you earn your first million, you will know that being rich is not just a privilege for a select few—it is a right you can obtain.

7

Wealth and Wisdom

"Wealth is the ability to fully experience life."
—Henry David Thoreau

An unorthodox doctor, who always thought beyond prescriptions, pills, and medication, once said to one of his regular patients, "I'm starting to suspect that the best medicine for humans is wisdom."

The surprised patient said, "What if wisdom doesn't work?"

The doctor smiled and said, "Increase the dose."

Wisdom allows us to understand life from God's perspective. Throughout the book of Proverbs, King Solomon encourages us to "get wisdom" (Proverbs 4:5). He says those who get wisdom love life (Proverbs 19:8); that it's better to get wisdom than gold (Proverbs 16:16); and that those who get wisdom find life and receive favor from the Lord (see 8:32–35).

In Ecclesiastes 7:23–24, Solomon also clarifies that getting wisdom is challenging: "'I am determined to be wise'—but this was beyond me. Whatever exists is far off and most profound—who can discover it?"

WHY THIS BOOK FROM THE BIBLE MADE ME MILLIONS

Wisdom and knowledge, both recurring themes in the Bible, are related but not synonymous. The Oxford dictionary defines wisdom as "the ability to discern or judge what is true, right, or lasting." Conversely, knowledge is "information gained through experience, reasoning, or acquaintance." Knowledge can exist without wisdom, but not the other way around. One can be knowledgeable without being wise. Knowledge is knowing how to use a gun; wisdom is knowing when to use it.

God wants us to have knowledge of Him and what He expects of us. In order to obey Him, we have to know His laws. Therefore, it is equally essential to have knowledge as it is to have wisdom.

James 1:5 states, "If any of you lacks wisdom, you should ask God, who gives generously to all without finding fault, and it will be given to you." God blesses us with wisdom for us to glorify Him.

Wisdom is the fitting application of knowledge. Knowledge understands the light has turned red; wisdom applies the brakes. Knowledge sees the quicksand; wisdom walks around it. Knowledge memorizes the Ten Commandments; wisdom obeys them. Knowledge learns of God; wisdom loves Him. Knowledge knows Scripture; wisdom puts it to use.

Suppose a man or woman possessing the qualifications and licensures to sell insurance went around calling themselves an agent but never taught anyone about the difference between term and life insurance or refused to help someone who needed their benefits. Would you say they operate as agents in their client's best interest? No, they just did enough to pass a test.

They are someone who has knowledge and potential—or rather, *wasted* knowledge and potential. The same applies to people who say they have knowledge and wisdom but don't apply it.

God intends for everyone to thrive economically. Therefore, he wants us to have provisions (basic needs) for our daily life. Furthermore, God's world has ample resources to provide all we need. However, in the fallen world we inhabit, many people fail to experience God's abundant provision.

Don't think for a moment longer that you still have to be broke and don't deserve the best financial resources available. Do not believe the lies that say you have to reach a certain level of success by a certain age or life is over for you. I failed to lift my head above water until I was forty-two. I questioned my self-worth countless times until I finally let go of everything that made me feel worthless and inadequate.

I doubted I measured up because I lacked education. I was ignorant about finances. I had a hard time finding my identity.

I was the only Filipino in the neighborhood filled with Polish, Greek, Black, Italian, and Latino people and never truly felt accept. As a result, I struggled with who I was for years.

Regarding finances, I wanted to provide but felt I was so far behind. Maybe you feel that way too. I had no background in sales or business, but the more I immersed myself in information and wisdom, the more I realized not everyone knew what I did. I had value to offer.

Living in abundance means seeking after God and His goodness. If your desires line up with God's will, He will look upon your request with favor and allow it to come to pass. We can't do anything to earn God's abundance. It is not an "if I manifest it, it will happen" kind of thing; however, I believe there are some things we can do on our behalf to position us to receive abundance.

FIVE BE'S OF ABUNDANCE

1. Be Diligent

Just putting in a little money here and there or when you feel like it ends up in little wealth. Be consistent when you invest money over the long term. Hunker down and work hard, no matter your feelings on a particular day. This action will pay off in the long run.

Most people have no investment plan and their lack of diligence shows. As a result, many of these people end up hungry, poor, in debt, and forced to work until they can't anymore.

2. Be Faithful

Luke 16:10-11: "Whoever can be trusted with very little can also be trusted with much, and whoever is dishonest with very little will also be dishonest with much."

The Bible tells us it's about faithful first, then rich (Proverbs 28:2). I didn't set out to get rich. I was faithful with the opportunities before me and disciplined in marketing daily and monthly. I followed up and helped people and asked for referrals. Guess what happened along the way? I got rich.

If you desire to build massive wealth, you first need to be trustworthy and disciplined with what you already have. You will never become wealthy if you're spending more than you make. You must be the master of your money before the Master can trust you with more.

3. Be Smart

Remember in 2 Corinthians 9:6-8 where it says, "Whoever sows sparingly will also reap sparingly, and whoever sows generously will also reap generously." Just like real seeds, money can't grow and produce more if you don't put it to work. Stowing your money in a savings account or under the mattress fails to build wealth.

When you invest money wisely, you produce more seeds that yield an even greater future harvest. With that said, please remember that some investments will fail to work out in your favor. However, keep sowing your seed into good ground and tending to it well; your harvest will be much greater than your losses.

Unfortunately, many people live on more than they make. When you spend more than you make, you have no seed to sow for a future harvest.

Money is nothing if you don't put it to work. Of course, keep a reserve on hand for an emergency, and have some to provide for your future, but beyond that, money should never be stagnant. It's easy for some people to think of saving and investing as a purely selfish act. But, when you do it right, it's a godly investing principle that benefits your life and the lives of others.

God is a limitless being who creates and multiplies. When He created us in His image, He also endowed us with these attributes. When you invest your money, you creatively multiply your money!

4. Be Prepared

The Bible teaches us this principle. For example, we see Joseph instructing Pharaoh to use the good years to prepare for the bad ones, and we see Noah putting food and animals on the ark before the flood.

I have learned that Mormons store an essential supply of items that will sustain life for several months and then a longer supply of the foods they ordinarily eat. For most of us, preparedness for natural disasters is something we acknowledge as important–and something we plan to do. "Eventually," we say, or "When I have the time, I'll get around to it." It might even be on our list of things to do. For a few of us, we might even have preparedness plans. Unfortunately, they're probably collecting dust somewhere on a shelf.

Preparing for adversity and being as self-reliant as possible in times of personal or widespread emergency allows you to be better. Self-reliance is an essential part of God's plan. It teaches us to be responsible people who work for what we need.

Preparation is the difference between success and failure, mediocrity and excellence, and average and above average. Someone once said, "One thing greater than the will to succeed is the will to prepare." Without preparation, failure is inevitable. Why are there so many leadership books and video lessons available—because we need to be prepared for the present and future.

Proverbs 30:25 says, "Ants are creatures of little strength, yet they store up their food in the summer." Have you ever seen a lazy ant? I've never seen a live ant just standing still, lying on the sofa, watching TV, or doing nothing. There are no "couch potato" ants. They are constantly moving.

They prepare with resilience. You can run over an anthill with a lawn mower, kick it in, or wash it away with a water hose, but before you know it, they'll build it back! It takes a lot to discourage an ant.

Ants don't know the meaning of procrastination! They don't wait until the weather turns cold before they begin to prepare. They gather food while it is still warm and take it into their colony. Many who work hard all day will never eat the food they prepare because they will die before cold weather, but they want to ensure that their families are taken care of even if they are not around. It only makes sense to ensure that our families will be taken care of in the future if something happens to us. That's just plain good common sense. They are future-oriented. They are not living in the past or just for the present. They are preparing for what lies ahead. They value preparation.

When you have a plan, you're not thrown off in panic and fear if something happens. Instead, you have confidence, clarity, and calmness.

On the other hand, if you don't plan, you have no reserve to draw from when hard times come, and you're forced to make desperate financial decisions. As Will Smith says, "It's best to stay ready, so you don't have to get ready." In other words, stay prepared!

5. Be Patient

Proverbs 13:11 says, "Wealth gained hastily will dwindle, but whoever gathers little by little will increase it." Patience is a good complement to being diligent. Building lasting wealth takes time. Imagine growing a mighty oak tree vs. planting tomatoes. When you plant tomatoes, you expect a relatively quick harvest that provides for a season, but an oak tree takes decades to become large and robust and will stand for generations to come.

So if you're looking at this book as a fast way to get rich, it won't happen. You can't treat faith in your Creator like a get-rich-quick overnight scheme. As a matter of fact, several verses talk about that.

Ecclesiastes 5:10 says, "Whoever loves money will never be satisfied with money. Whoever loves wealth will never be satisfied with more income." King Solomon said this in the latter years, looking back at his lavish life.

Imagine having a life where any decision you have to make, money is no longer a variable in the equation of making decisions. You are at a place where you can remove money from the decision.

Even while writing this book, I don't think about groceries, inflation, and rising interest rates anymore because money is not a factor for me. I am grateful that I am not affected by it and that my family and I can continue to operate and help others.

However, I am not desensitized to the needs of those who can't take care of themselves. I fully understand that people are in need. If generations implemented the information I'm sharing in this book, families would have money to help those who need additional care instead of setting up GoFundMe accounts and hoping people contribute.

God has put more significant things in my life than money; again it is only part of the equation. I'm working right now to ensure that money's not an equation for big decisions because I want to contribute to ministries and churches. I want to build schools, finance non-profit organizations, and produce movies. Guess what I need? Money.

A deep recession has been brewing inside our country. It will be more difficult for those realtors and loan officers I've worked with for at least the next two years. I saw what happened to my friends in this type of industry during the dot.com bubble of 2001 and the Great Recession of 2007-2009. It wasn't pretty.

We choose life insurance policies and indexed annuities that would help anticipate losses and offer minimum guarantees regardless of what happens to the economy.

The government hasn't officially announced the recession of 2022, yet it has already impacted many people. People are at risk of losing money in their 401(k) plans and retirement plans. The equity built up in their home will be at risk. Inflation of 9.1% was reported today in July 2022, and the Federal Reserve still has plans to increase interest rates.

Since I've sought wisdom—the same wisdom I am sharing with you—my team and clients haven't lost any money based on the products and services we offer. We choose life insurance policies and indexed annuities that would help anticipate losses and offer minimum guarantees regardless of what happens to the economy.

MADE BANK ON THE BENTLEY

Years ago, a friend of mine was in real estate during the Great Recession. He was having a rough year that resulted in a massive financial reversal. He just bought a brand-new Bentley GT, Continental and only had it a few weeks. Unfortunately, he was also going through a nasty divorce around the same time. He reached out to me for what I thought would be an encouraging and supportive word.

"Matt, I just bought this car all-cash. I need money. I can't wait for the dealership to open. I'm willing to suck it up and take a steep hit. But I need money right now—like tonight."

The urgency and panic in his voice caused me not to ask any questions about why he needed the money.

Trying to help, I responded, "Okay, what do you want for it?"

He said, "Listen, Matt, I get it. I'm going to feel the pain, but make me an offer. Insult me. I just need money right now."

"Insult you? Okay." The car was roughly $110k. He confirmed he just wanted an offer. "I can do $50k."

"Come on, Matt, come on," He pleaded. "Man, can you at least give me 70k?"

"You told me to insult you," I continued. "I tell you what, if you meet me at Chase Bank at the grocery store, halfway between our houses, I'll give you $60k."

Surprisingly he agreed.

I went to meet him. After he confirmed he had the title with him, I looked at the bank teller and requested, "Can you cut him a certified check for $60k, please?" My friend's dad came with him and he was shaking his head the whole time.

Now, I get the pink title for a Bentley GT. I'm a single dad of three kids. What am I going to do with a convertible, two-seater? I knew exactly what I'd do. I would use it for a weekend car for nights out on the town. Would I be Money Smart Guy if I did that? I wanted to be a responsible father, so I did the next best thing—I listed it on Auto Trader for $100k. In no time, I had multiple offers. Finally, I settled for a cash offer at $95k. So my $60k turned into $95k.

A few weeks later, I did a financial review with a client. We were doing a 401(k) rollover because he was worried about the stock market crash and wanted to protect himself.

In the middle of completing an application for an index annuity, he looked over at me and inquired, "Matt, do you know anybody who wants to buy a townhouse? I need to move my great aunt into a nursing home. I'm the only family member that's around. I'm not able to care for her the way she needs to be cared for."

"No one comes to mind. What do you want for it? Where is it?"

"It's on Harlem and North Avenue."

"Oh, is that by the college?"

"Yep, it's right by the college."

Right away, I thought this would be a great opportunity. I can potentially get this townhouse and rent it to a bunch of college students.

So I said, "Let me get the address, and I'll take a look at it."

He replied, "Okay, but just know it hasn't been updated since the 1970s."

After looking at it, the townhome did have old bathrooms and finishings, but it had a solid foundation. Well, remember the cash from the GT? So I took another $5,000, $7,000, and gave the townhouse an HGTV makeover. I had the kitchen and bathroom gutted and replaced the 70s fixtures with updated ones. Within sixty days, I sold it for roughly $130,000.

Quick recap: I took $60k and bought the Bentley; then I made $30k from selling the Bentley for $90K. Afterward, I bought the townhouse and invested an additional $5-7k in it to get $130k. That's what happens when you're prepared.

I then used the profit fund to finance my insurance business operations. I ended up getting involved in other real estate opportunities. I got involved in other investment opportunities so I could have some cash. It took me years to save up the $50k but less than six months to turn that $60k into $130k because preparation met opportunity.

The Bentley was the opportunity. It wasn't in a currently crashing stock waiting on dividends or capital gains. Be open to "becoming your own bank" so you can take advantage of opportunities when they come your way.

If you're looking to plan for retirement with just cash in the bank, you're going to get crushed. Every day your money buys you less and less due to inflation.

Based on this month's CPI index report, they said that inflation is now up to 9.1%, up from 8.3%.[5] So if you got 1% in your savings account, when you use the old rule that many people know in the financial services world—the rule of 72, you divide your interest rate into 72. So that will effectively tell you when your money will double.

So if you divide 1% into 72, it will take 72 years for $10k to double to $20k. So your $10k will give you an increase of $10k in 72 years. Do the math—if it were only .5%, it'd take 144 years for your money to double.

Investing to make your money work for you is not necessarily about just a return in investments as it relates to the stock market or a 401(k). Investing means growing the capacity to obtain knowledge. It is about creating an experience or being around experienced people to gain wisdom. That's what investing money will do for you.

Look at the ripple effect of how much you can exceed inflation by having wisdom and knowledge. One decision can ripple effect your situation into one of abundance.

THE BEST INVESTMENT

I often get asked what my best investment has been. My answer? My best investment was in me! I invested books, courses, mastermind groups, weekly accountability, mentorship, events, and conferences into myself. I had to equip myself with the knowledge and wisdom by being around other people who have been

[5]CPI for all items rises 1.3% in June; gasoline, shelter, food indexes rise, June 2022

there and done that. I would ask them what they would do if they found themselves in a similar situation.

What would you have done differently with this situation if you had the money? I love when people ask me that question. That's probably the most effective way to tap into someone's wisdom.

I hope you understand that the first thing you have to invest in is yourself. Then, you elevate the value and condition of your spirit, mind, and heart. It's less about head knowledge and more about heart knowledge. Learning money moves are relatively easy and not as complicated as some financial experts lead you to believe

Another excellent investment I made was with my Rolls-Royce. I bought it from a former NBA player who finished playing in the league and had to sell off all of his toys.

Today this Rolls-Royce is twelve years old, and they're still offering me the same price I paid for it. So be sure to check out my YouTube video: "How I bought a Rolls-Royce and paid $24 a month for it."

HOW I BOUGHT A ROLLS ROYCE

I prepared and invested in the right financial tools and advisors. I talked to my CPA about how to have this car in service for my business so I can create the tax deductions for it. Select the QR code to watch the full video of how I did this.

My monthly payments, car depreciation, maintence, and upkeep were all deductible. So my net payment after tax deductions was $24. People pay more for coffee than I paid for my net payment from driving around with my Rolls-Royce.

INHERITANCE

Proverbs 13:22 says, "A good man leaves an inheritance to his children's children." Not just to your children, but your children's children.

By Filipino tradition, the oldest takes care of the youngest. The next oldest takes care of the next youngest, and so on. What happens if the oldest doesn't really want to do that? What chain reaction does this create throughout the rest of the siblings, the aging parents?

Now, I felt incumbent to do it even though my parents never told me, "You're the oldest. You got to do this."

I just felt it made sense for me to be responsible. I need to be the example. I need to take care of my sister. I need to take care of my parents. So I took that on, right?

However, my trust fund, the one my wife and I set up after spending hours with our lawyer, discussed how we distribute the money amongst our kids.

So I know my kids or their friends will probably read this book. Surprise! If you didn't already know, now you do. It is just a reminder.

When it comes to getting money from our family trust fund, I operate as God did with the Israelites. I believe in equal opportunity, not equal distribution. Not everyone will receive the same money when I go home to Heaven.

In order words, if my kids are not productive and earning income, they can expect to get little to nothing from the Sapaula Family Trust Fund. However, if you are gainfully employed and contributing to society instead of leaning on it, you are in good standing to receive income from our trust fund.

I believe that income is just a reflection of impact. If you are doing something positive, your income should reflect it. If you make a more substantial impact with your words and work, excellent, then the trust fund will reward you for such.

I don't want my kids to wait until I'm dead for them to say, "Oh, finally, we're getting some inheritance from my dad." I want to be able to give them counsel and invest in their endeavors. Unlike an institutional bank, my kids have to meet different criteria for us to invest in their endeavors or extend our support. If you do right, possess the right attitude, call me and ask for wisdom in your life, not just for money for your current need, and you are aligned with our family values, I want to finance or help elevate your business idea. I want to finance your education or certifications *now*. I'll help you with your car, apartment, or whatever you are doing *now*.

But if you don't do anything, fail to align with the family principles, and don't honor your family, I will not help you. Again, it's about an idea, impact, and life; they all must matter to you first. Everything is earned.

No one ever values much what they get for free. This may sound callous, but I'm giving them something I never got in my generation. I did not have someone with experience and money willing to back me up with any of my ideas. It never crossed my mind. I want my children to learn the value of earning things.

As obvious as it sounds, we can never run out of room for wisdom. God makes it available in unlimited supply and ever-increasing measures if you continue to pursue it throughout your life. So no matter how much wisdom you have, there's always room for more!

When you boil down these biblical investing principles to their essence, there is one overarching reason God wants to provide you with material wealth. It's so you can be a giver. I know it sounds counterintuitive, but when you give a portion of your wealth away, it's a natural law that it will come back to you multiplied.

Ultimately, it's not about you or your bank account; it's about how you can use material wealth to help yourself, your family, and others by funding projects that further God's kingdom and influence here on Earth.

8

Freedom Starts with Cash Flow

"You will never know true freedom until you achieve financial freedom."

— **Robert T. Kiyosaki**

Solomon, the richest and wisest king, says, "A feast is made for laughter, wine makes merry; but money answers everything" (Ecclesiastes 10:19). At some point in your life, you've probably heard someone say, "I don't care about money." You may have even said that yourself. While this sentiment sounds nice in theory, the reality is that money is of great importance for four main reasons.

- **Money gives you freedom**. When you have enough money, you can live where you want, take care of your needs, and indulge in your hobbies and passions. Suppose you are able to become financially independent and have the financial resources necessary to live on without working. In that case, you'll enjoy even more freedom since you will be able to do what you want with your time.

- **Money gives you the power to pursue your dreams.** Having money makes it possible for you to start a business, build a dream home, invest in the costs of having a family, plan for the future, or accomplish other goals.
- **Money gives you security.** When you have enough money working for you, you'll never need to worry about having a roof over your head, having enough to eat, or seeing a doctor when you're sick. You have the opportunity to have what you desire, but you'll have to work for it.
- **Money gives you access.** Money gets you access to pretty much anything you want or need. It gives you access to certain people and high-level conversations. If you wish to take care of your aging parents, money can make that happen. I was even able to reverse the adverse effects of the military and sports injuries I incurred because I had access to resources to relieve the pain I experienced.

Unfortunately, many people fail to live this way. I have always said whoever controls your income controls you; therefore, you don't have freedom, power, security, or access if you aren't creating a way to be your own bank.

As the saying goes, "They have more month than they do money." As soon as they earn a dime, they spend a quarter. There's nothing carried forward. They aren't the only ones. I did this too—for far too long.

I remember having the mentality of not wanting to screw things up again because filing bankruptcy weighed heavily on me. Why did I file bankruptcy? I spent more than I brought in. I was $20k in credit card debt, and I only made $20k a year as a sergeant in the Marines, gross pay. The only way I could make more money in the Marines was to go on deployments and join the combat zone. What a great way to make more money.

Again, I'm not a financial advisor, but I suggest asking your financial advisor some questions about what I'm fixing to discuss with you.

Everyone is not in a bad financial situation. If they were, there would be no way for five million people to become millionaires across the world despite the economic damage from COVID. While many poor became poorer, the number of millionaires increased by 5.2 million to 56.1 million globally.[6]

In 2020, more than 1% of all adults worldwide will become millionaires for the very first time. There are just over 21,951,000 millionaires in the U.S., according to the latest Global Wealth Report from the Credit Suisse Research Institute.[7] The U.S. had the greatest year-over-year growth of any nation in the number of millionaires within its borders. Worldwide, the number of millionaires had increased to 56.1 million, marking a significant rise from the year before when there were only

[6]BBC News, Millions become millionaires during Covid pandemic, June 2021
[7]Investopedia, The Number of Millionaires Continues to Increase, Charlotte Wold, Updated January 2022

50.8 million millionaires. The forecast for the number of millionaires in 2025 is to exceed 84 million.[8]

When you don't save and invest, it is like telling the Big Man Upstairs that you have no faith and are better off controlling everything yourself and He doesn't have the power to improve your situation. You believe more in the natural than the promise of the supernatural.

COUNTRY FOUNDED ON CAPITALISM

The country has been under lockdown protocols, coronavirus scare tactics—mask, unmask, vaccinate, don't vaccinate, social distancing, etc., from 2020-2022. In the meantime, the country has actually spent a lot of money, pouring it out to its citizens.

Capitalism is not a contrivance: it is a manifestation of nature. No person, committee, or nation invented it. They didn't have to—it just happens naturally as an essential means of survival and advancement. The same is true for entrepreneurialism.

Freedom is our natural state as humans; free-market capitalism is its natural manifestation. The wealth of individuals, communities, and nations comes first from the world of business, where producers and consumers of goods and services meet in free, mutually rewarding exchanges. Everyone benefits from the natural and necessary fruits of capitalism. Even freedom-depriving systems such as socialism, communism, and dictatorships must release strong enough doses of capitalism to keep their economies (and people) alive.

[8]Jenny McCall, Number of global millionaires to grow significantly, June 2021

More money has been printed—over 2.2 trillion dollars is in circulation as of June 2022. Federal stimulus plans were an emergency monetary policy to protect our economy from the COVID-19 pandemic. Since March 2020, the Federal Reserve has bought $80 billion in treasuries and $40 billion in housing-backed securities each month. As a result, the Fed's balance sheet has swelled to $8.6 trillion from $4.4 trillion.[9]

The government has just printed a massive amount of money in the last couple of years. Some sources say that since January 2020, the US has printed nearly 80% of all US dollars ever in history.

How much is $1 trillion? Here are two examples to put it into perspective.

1. It would take you 31,710 years to count from one to $1 trillion.
2. If you spent $1 million a day since Jesus was born over 2,022 years ago, you would have only spent just a little over $2.7 billion.

So if that is the case with money printed in America, everybody just got richer, right? Wrong! I'm already stepping on a few toes, so I won't discuss politics a great deal—but we all know people vote based on who they believe would benefit them.

The government does a phenomenal job of selling a dream and making promises, but delivering and making good on their word is another story—or book for another day. A good chunk of the trillion dollars has not filtered down to the American people. At times, people were making more money sitting at

[9]By Lindsay Dunsmuir, Explainer: Federal Reserve's taper: How does it work?, November 2021

home and collecting unemployment checks, stimulus checks, and child tax credit checks than at work.

Cash flow is the money that comes into your business minus the money that leaves. It's a part of your CPA prepared financials and is usually shown in a separate cash flow statement. Yet cash flow is more than an accounting exercise. It's a key indicator of financial health.

Without strong cash flow, you can't pay your bills, plan for the future, or serve others in a greater capacity. Therefore, capital asset purchases and proceeds from selling and buying investments are great investments to increase your cash flow. Financing activities include all proceeds from financial institutions, investors, and shareholders, reflecting long-term debt, line-of-credit payments, and distributions.

Cash flow helps you expand, make large purchases, or invest. In addition, it gives outside parties, such as a surety, bank, or investor, a good way to measure your future earning power.

Over the last few years, the government has competed not only with employers but with the universal principle that for us to value something, we have to work for it. I've realized the rich are being vilified, and the poor are idealized as though the latter is better. The people who don't have money are the ones who resent the rich.

It doesn't make sense to reward the poor by taxing the performers, innovators, risk-takers, job creators, and entrepreneurs.

Instead, those who are willing to get uncomfortable and sacrifice are the ones who should be rewarded.

Capitalism changed my life by creating conditions where an immigrant, first-generation Filipino-American kid with no money, credit, college degree, or business experience could make a $500 investment and build an $85 million company in less than six years.[10] Just as profit enables and feeds the lives of individuals, it manifests capitalism as the fountainhead of civilization.

Capitalism-borne freedom and civilization enable and amplify the shared happiness, peace of mind, and compassion that hold people together.

Like the governments of all other modern democracies, the United States government redistributes the incomes of its citizens on a massive scale. The American public generally supports such redistribution in principle, understanding that it is intended to help the poor. The lives of the needy, the argument goes, would be far worse without this aid, and presumably, such redistribution is designed to avoid undue harm to everyone else.

Whether one agrees with it or not, this popular understanding of redistribution's purpose yields some concern to the people who have obtained financial freedom. The aim of helping the poor is commendable; however, poverty could decrease if people taught generational wealth to their children and their

[10]Daniel Levi, 80% of all US dollars in existence were printed in the last 22 months (from $4 trillion in January 2020 to $20 trillion in October 2021)

children's children. The means of redistribution confirms that the rich get richer while the poor get poor because their financial decisions are not getting them further than where they started.

Before my wife and I got married, we had a conversation about financial freedom. At that time, we were raising our blended family of four—seriously dating with marriage right around the corner.

I asked her, "When did you start feeling financial freedom?"

After a brief pause, she responded, "When we made $250k."

I thought she was going to say at least $500k.

I processed her response and inquired, "Why that amount?"

She replied, "Because I stopped looking at the right side of the menu."

Intrigued, I asked, "What do you mean?"

"We could go to the restaurant without worrying about the right side of the menu. We could focus on enjoying a meal instead of looking at the price. We could get an appetizer, salad, entree, dessert, and whatever we'd like without having to glance at the amount it would cost," she explained.

"We could bless the server with a great tip," I added.

What can I say? The time I spent as a server at Olive Garden stuck with me. I enjoy looking for ways to give to those who serve.

That was the beginning of freedom. We could go to Whole Foods without it costing an entire paycheck. We were able to invest in our health. The food we were putting in our bodies drastically changed then.

Now we may not have been traveling all over the world or buying our dream cars that we wanted to drive, but we were headed in the right direction.

When we retired our parents, we began experiencing family freedom at a $500k income. We were able to help those we love and care about. Not only did we take care of our children, but we could also take care of both sets of parents and give them stipends to help them financially. As a result, they wouldn't have to pay for anything for the rest of their lives. They gave us life and the opportunity when they were our age, and it was time for us to contribute back to them.

When we made $750k, we had obtained status, which meant we could go to any restaurant and park valet. Instead of just going to a concert, we took advantage of purchasing the best seats. Instead of just going to church, we could significantly contribute to helping those in need.

Many people made more money staying at home living off government checks through the pandemic than they did, sticking with their jobs if they could.

For the last two years, we have had a shot at financially leveling up the middle class. Sadly, most people blew it. When the lockdown happened, my team shared a Tweet stating, "You'll either learn a new skill or habit that will make you money. If not, you just have to realize you were just lazy."

The New York Times reported over six million people had left their jobs, leaving over eleven billion jobs available.[11] Online streaming services exploded in new subscribers. Netflix had a record 36 million subscribers in 2020. The last two years caused a bunch of laziness and cockiness in many people. It triggered an era called "the Great Resignation."

People had access to use their 401(k) plan during the pandemic—without the 10% early withdrawal penalties for withdrawing before 59.5 years old. It was probably the best thing for them to have money saved up in their 401(k) plan; otherwise, they would have spent it all or not had anything to begin with.

Capital and credit have been accessible, but what do most have to show for it? Absolutely nothing! The rich got richer, the poor got even poorer, but those in the middle class who prepared and took action got richer, too.

Sadly, 68% of all people in the US are living paycheck to paycheck.[12] According to the reports, this number is steadily increased. In addition, the number of people earning more than $100,000 and $250,000 per year who reported living pay-

---

[11]Ben Casselman, Highest Record of U.S. Workers Quitting, November 2021

[12]Jessica Dickler, CNBC, Life Changes, Americans Living Paycheck to Paycheck, March 2022

check to paycheck has also increased. So money alone, plus savings alone, will not help you advance financially. So what will?

If you look at what faith and farmers have in common, they know they have to do the work to cultivate the land, plant, and water the seeds, be patient with the seeds, take care of the land, watch these seeds grow, and refrain from harvesting early.

As soon as your seeds start to show growth by sticking out of the ground, you don't cut them down right away. You don't see one apple, banana, or coconut on a tree and rush to consume it. But, sadly, that's what people do with their money.

If people spent some of this stimulus money on something needed instead of rushing to get something they wanted, they would be further ahead. You lack discipline if you didn't come out of the lockdown with a new skillset or higher learning. For a brief period, the world stopped. Time and money were on our side. The time at home should have allowed everyone to have a greater appreciation of learning new skills.

People say, "Cash is king." After consulting with many people in business and dealing with it myself, I've discovered cash *flow* is king, if you're like me, who didn't have cash, to begin with. While cash flow is king, excellent credit is queen, and cash just sitting in the bank—with no plans to do anything with it—is for jokers.

3 C'S OF MONEY

Everything starts with cash flow. If you don't have a large cash flow, it's important to improve your skillset; in exchange, you get paid more. The saying goes, "The more you learn, the more you earn." I believe that's true, but I created and adopted the mindset of, "The more you evolve, the more problems you solve."

3 C'S OF MONEY

The more problems you can solve, the higher value you create for yourself at your job or in the marketplace. More people want to be associated with you, hire you, or align with you.

I'm going to share a brief overview of the 3 C's of Money, but you can click on the QR code so you can go more in-depth on how to build wealth.

1. Cash Flow: The source that cannot stop flowing in case of emergencies, setbacks, and tough times.
2. Credit: You need excellent credit (720-850) and establish credit history.
3. Capital: This is savings for reinvestments.

I incorporated the 50-30-20 rule, which helped me get out of debt and how I manage money. I separate 20% for tithes, charitable contributions, and taxes. I use 30% percent for savings and investments, and live off of the remaining 50%.

Some of you may automatically say, "I can't live off 50% of my income!" You're right. If you're in this situation, you've spent your way into a financial corner. The only way out of it is two ways. Cut your expenses and reduce your lifestyle. Or you can find ways to increase your income.

One will cause you to buy into your fears, settle for what you have, and shut off your dream machine. The other will put fire in your belly, exercise that faith you've been praying about, and watch the heavens open doors you never thought would appear in your lifetime.

SYSTEM FOR MAKING FINANCIAL DECISIONS

Oftentimes, when families and friends get together, they argue, discuss, and even debate where to put their money because people are defensive about their finances. When emotions are high, guess what happens? Logic is down.

In 2005, I started learning insurance strategies called Infinite Banking, Be Your Own Banker, Life Insurance Retirement Plan, etc,. I received information from a mentor, NY Timesbest-selling author, Douglas Andrew. He illustrated the L.S.R.T system along with the Four Homes of Money. I still use this system to determine how I invest money. This helps me process and see things clearly because it takes away all the emotions.

Money needs somewhere to go. It needs a home, right? But in order for me to choose the right place for it to go, I need to do my due diligence and homework so I can make the best choice.

L.S.R.T. TEST

Serious money is money you can count on and funds you know will be there at a later date. In this investment system, I use what I call an L.S.R.T. test. This allows me to create a system for saving time, energy, and money and keeping relationships healthy, fruitful, and intact. It helps me make a more educated and informed decision.

When somebody pitches me an idea of where to put my money, I run it through this filter; therefore, I'm less emotional and more thoughtful and logical when deciding. Let's break down this formula and then we will discuss the Four Homes of Money and put each one to the test.

L stands for liquidity. I want my money accessible in a relatively short period of time. So if I have my money earning a particular rate of return and let it marinate there for a period of months or years, I want to make sure I can access it with an 800 number or EFT transfer in a day or two, so it goes right back into my bank account.

S stands for safety. I want my money safe and to avoid losses. I don't want to worry about my money spiraling downward while I'm in the middle of a meeting or during quality time spent with my family. I don't want to look over my back. I don't want it exposed to losses based on wars, economic crises, or bad decisions made in the White House. I want my money to be there.

If you suffer a 10% loss, you'll need a 12% gain the next year just to get you back to where you started. If you suffered a 50% loss, you'd need a 100% gain the next year to get you back to where you started. Suffering losses comes with emotional anguish and requires additional time and patience to reach your financial goals.

R is for rate of return. I want my money to earn a rate of return that outpaces inflation, increases my purchasing power, and has uninterrupted compounding growth over time.

T is for tax advantages. When I pull my money out, I don't want Uncle Sam, any state, or the IRS having a say about how much money I can keep. So I prefer to either minimize or eliminate what I have to must pay in federal and/or state income tax.

So now that we've talked about how to assess how to decide where our money goes, let's break down "The Four Homes of Money" and why they are important:

BANKS — Banks are a great place to send your direct deposits. However, no one will become wealthy, earning the meager low rates of return banks traditionally offer. Plus, your earnings will be taxable if your savings account, money market, or CD is not in a qualified retirement plan.

STOCK MARKET — Many people have participated in the stock market through their company's qualified retirement plans. Whether it be a 401k for a for-profit corporation, 403(b) for a non-profit; a 457 or deferred compensation plan for a state and municipality; and a TSP, a thrift savings plan for federal government employees (stock market), I'd even include crypto and foreign exchange currency in this broad category.

REAL ESTATE — This is property consisting of land or buildings that you own. So may call this "brick and mortar" and/or a real, tangible asset.

LIFE INSURANCE RETIREMENT PLAN (LIRP) — These aren't typical policies you get through your employer. They are acquired directly from the life insurance company as a private, not employer-based, policy. It is designed to stay in force for your entire life while potentially building significant cash value credited through dividends, interest rate credits, or growth indirectly connected to a stock market index, like the S&P 500, without any downside risk.

Courtesy of @Europa26

If it's been a while since you asked yourself where you should keep your money, it might be time to mix it up. Whether you want to keep your cash accessible or save it and let it grow, there are several places you can put your money because it needs a home.

Let's run these homes of money through the L.S.R.T. test of liquidity, safety, rate of return, and tax advantages so you can decide where you need to put your money.

BANKS

Is it liquid? Yes.

You put my money in, and then I can take it out, whether it be a bank CD, money market, or savings account. For CDs, I have to marinate it there for a year or two or three or five years, depending on how long that bank CD period is. However, if I pull my money out beforehand, federal law sets a minimum penalty on early withdrawals from CDs, but there is no maximum. But for the most part, money inside banks is liquid, including checking, savings, and money market accounts.

Is it safe? Yes.

You get the interest rate as promised. However, if the bank goes bankrupt or into receivership, the FDIC (Federal Deposit Insurance Corporation) covers accounts up to $250,000.

Does it have a rate of return? No.

Money in banks doesn't typically earn a rate of return in the bank. So why did I say no? Are you excited about making historically low-interest rates with the average one-year CD yield of .19% or an average five-year CD yield of .36%?

Meanwhile, the consumer price index, a broad measure of everyday goods and services related to the cost of living, increased 9.1% from June 2021 to June 2022. Let's round up to one percent for CD. Does this fire you up to open up a CD right now? Probably not. Maybe back in the 70s and 80s, when inflation was the highest, people were getting double-digit returns on their CDs, but that was fifty years ago. The banks are paying a meager interest rate; therefore, you have a poor rate of return on your money.

Does it have a tax advantage? No.

If I put my money in a savings account and it's earning an interest rate, a money market account, or a CD, I'll have to pay income taxes because I have to address the 1099-INT for disclosing the interest earned. So you have to add that interest to your income and pay income tax on it. I'd say it's kind of a slap in the face.

If I have $10,000 that earns a 0.5% interest rate, I'll owe taxes on $50 that I earned. So I have to add that to my adjusted gross income, in which I pay income taxes on the money I made in the bank. Are you good with that?

STOCK MARKET

The next home for money could be the stock market, within a 401k qualified retirement plan. Many people find this a convenient way to save for retirement because it can be automatically deducted from their paycheck. They don't see this as another withdrawal from their bank account after receiving your take-home pay.

Is it liquid? No.

You have to be 59.5 years old to withdraw this money. If you do, you will have to pay a 10% early withdrawal penalty and pay federal and state income tax on the amount you withdraw. You can loan from your 401(k) plan to bypass these penalties and taxes; however, if you do not repay this loan, these taxes and penalties will be applied.

Is it safe? Not completely.

It depends on how you allocate your funds to invest within the plan. If you try to swing for the fences, your money is exposed to losses and potential gains. On the other hand, when you are defensive with your money and put it into cash and/or cash equivalents, you have to cross your fingers and hope your money beats the inflation rate.

Keep this in mind, where there is no ceiling, there's also no basement. You can earn a lot of money, but in any given year, at any given moment, you can also lose a lot of money if your money is not allocated properly. And there's no way to predict a stock market crash while you're busy at your job, running your business, and raising your family.

As well-equipped as these 401(k) plan administrators are to educate their clients, it is incumbent upon the clients themselves to ask plenty of questions and increase their level of financial literacy.

When it is time to retire, you don't want the stock market to drop and cause your income to drop proportionally. But, I witnessed during the 2001 Recession and the Great Recession of 2008-2009, so many were hurt by the money they thought would be there, and it wasn't.

Does it have a rate of return? Yes.

When there is growth in the stock market, and your money is allocated to this growth, you will see potential gains.

Anytime you place money in an investment, you should receive a prospectus that describes the nature of the offering. It is a legal disclosure that provides information that a person can use to make an informed investment decision. Unfortunately, at the front of many prospectuses, I have always received a disclosure summarizing that I could lose money.

Does it have tax advantages? Yes and no.

It is tax-advantaged or not taxed when your money accumulates and grows. However, when you withdraw this money from your retirement account, that's when the tax man cometh.

In other words, Uncle Sam lets you grow your money tree over the accumulation and contribution phase of your working years. Then, when it's time to harvest for the distribution phase of your life in retirement, that's when the federal income taxes will be paid.

Since I'm a new Texas resident and around more farmland than I was in Chicago, let me use this analogy.

Would you rather be taxed on your penny seeds in the spring or your million-dollar harvest in the fall? I presume many of you would rather be taxed on your penny seeds because you don't know how big your million-dollar harvest will be.

Well, the opposite is happening inside any qualified retirement plan your employer offers. So the homes of money are based on my L.S.R.T test. What do I have? There is no liquidity; half are unsafe, half have a decent rate of return and half have a tax advantage.

REAL ESTATE

Is it liquid? No.

The only way you get money out of real estate is two ways, assuming this is your personal residence. First, you either refinance your property so you can cash out your equity. Or you sell the property minus the costs, fees, commissions, and expenses of the transaction minus what you owe to the mortgage company at closing.

Then the proceeds are now your cash in hand. That's how you liquidate your money out of your home. Either you cash out, refinance, or you sell the property.

Is it safe? Yes and no.

It all depends on your zip code. The area you live in may drop based on the local community real estate value. So you could potentially lose money inside real estate in terms of value.

At the release of this book in August 2022, there was a massive rise in property values over the last fourteen years, dating back to 2007-2009.

A simple search on the realtor.com app shows many "price reduced" properties for sale when many homes were selling above the original listed price a year ago. This reflects homes losing value and retracting due to less demand. In addition, the Federal Reserve has been raising interest rates to combat a crippling inflation rate only seen this high since the 1980s.

Does it have a rate of return? Yes and no.

Again, it depends on your zip code and whether there are foreclosures and like-kind properties selling lower or higher than fair market value. However, there can be a decent rate of return in terms of value appreciation and equity built up as your pay down your mortgage.

I clearly remember during the 2000s when everyone was getting into real estate. They would say that the prices would always go up and everyone would always pay their mortgage before anything else." Sadly, we found out that wasn't true, triggering the Great Recession, where many people had property values underwater. Many found themselves owing more money on the mortgage than the property was worth.

Does it have tax advantages? Yes.

Whether you're real estate investing or you live in your home as a primary residence, real estate has some significant tax advantages. For example, if you are single and have a capital gain in your primary residence up to $250,000, there is no capital gain tax. In addition, married couples enjoy up to a $500,000 exemption from capital gains tax.

If you invest in real estate aside from your primary residence, you may sell that property and replace it with another like-kind property. As a result, it will defer the payment of any capital gains tax that would usually be due.

So does it pass completely my four filters? Liquidity? No. Safety? Yes and no. Rate of return? Yes and no. And tax advantages? Yes. It seems to be about the same as the previous homes. Not one yet has checked off all the boxes.

Thankfully this isn't House Hunters on HGTV, where you have to choose from three houses. There is another category to house your money, but most people don't know about it. Is it possible there is something with liquidity, safety, rate of return, and tax advantages all in one financial home? Let's find out.

LIFE INSURANCE RETIREMENT PLAN (LIRP)

The fourth home of money is not the stock market, real estate market, or bank market; it is the life insurance industry.

Life insurance is not just for death. Life insurance is for life. It is for living. It's a selfless act. People buy life insurance because they love their family and spouse, and they want to make sure that somebody they love is financially prepared and taken care of long after they've passed away.

Furthermore, life insurance has a significant tax-advantaged haven for your money to grow and accumulate. If you need benefits from the policy or policies you may obtain, you might not ever have to pay a dime in income tax. Let me go over this again.

Life insurance retirement plans, or LIRPs, are an insurance strategy using a permanent life insurance policy such as whole life, universal life, and indexed universal life. Term insurance, which is always viewed as the most inexpensive, does not build cash value and is not used as a home for money.

Is it liquid? Yes.

You can either take a loan or withdraw from these policies with no early penalties. You can access your cash if there is a net cash surrender value in the policy. You'll have to ask a properly trained life insurance agent who can appropriately structure this policy according to IRS tax codes. Contrary to popular belief, you can adequately and appropriately take money out of the policy without triggering surrender charge penalties.

You can either minimize, mitigate, or eliminate some early withdrawal provisions by understanding the loan withdrawal provision. But for the most part, you have the option to take money out of a life insurance policy. You don't have to die to use it.

I've personally used cash value from these policies, and money inside this insurance strategy, to purchase real estate and luxury cars under my business. Why would I do this? To keep from paying interest to financial institutions. This is part of a "be your own bank" strategy that I will outline in later work so that I don't pay interest to another financial institution unless I want to.

Is it safe? Yes.

Based on the stock market drop, specific policies, whether whole life, universal life, or index universal life, have minimum guarantees. However, most people look at life insurance policies for one reason, only for a funeral or the loss of a loved one.

Listen, life insurance has more styles and uses than just death. After all, it's called *life* insurance, and there are many ways to use it during your lifetime.

Insurance can't be placed in one category since it can be used for many different purposes. It's an asset class, and thanks to capitalism, competition, and the growth of the life insurance industry, there are more policies in the life insurance industry that have been developed since the 1980s. Many of the modern permanent life insurance policies today are specifically designed to help one in the retirement planning process, which means you can be in a position where you don't lose capital.

I now own almost a dozen policies over the past twenty years. In addition, my wife and all five kids have their policies set up for more than just funeral expenses.

Plus, I have not had any losses in my cash value from stock market conditions, economic changes, two significant recessions, and a pandemic. I am looking to obtain even more policies with an exponentially growing business.

Does it have a rate of return? Yes.

For purposes of this book, the variable universal life insurance policy is not included in this question. Although it can potentially earn a high upside rate of return, it is directly affected by the stock market. Therefore, selecting a safe money strategy would not be an appropriate "safe money" policy.

With that said, the other permanent life insurance policies mentioned previously were whole, universal, and indexed universal life. The cash value grows inside the policy based on dividends, fixed interest, and index interest based on an index such as the S&P 500, respectively.

Does it have tax advantages? Yes.

A significant advantage of life insurance is using Internal Revenue Code sections 101(a), 72(e), and 7702. Using a

FOUR HOMES OF MONEY

combination of these tax codes allows you to grow money within a permanent life insurance policy. You can smartly grow, access, and pass on money from an insurance policy without paying a dime in taxes. The wealthy have been doing this for generations.

Now that we've gotten through the L.S.R.T. and the four homes of money, where would you rather see your safe money grow? For simplicity purposes, check off the boxes in the illustration as you go through this process.

Please send me a Tweet @MoneySmartGuy or tag me on IG with what you came up with for your answer using #FaithMadeMillionaire.

I uploaded a video on my YouTube channel showing a couple of case studies. Many entrepreneurs pulled money from their life insurance policy to fund their businesses and build their dream, and today, some are even publicly traded. They are Walt Disney, Ray Kroc of McDonald's, JC Penney, and even Master P.

Here's another use for life insurance. Let's say Grandma wanted to leave you $50k in cash. Well, if your seventy-year-old grandmother could qualify for a life insurance policy, that $50k potentially be turned into a $100k life insurance policy.

You don't leave cash by itself as a financial inheritance. Instead, you leave that cash inside a life insurance policy, assuming you can qualify for it based on health underwriting requirements.

HOW WAKA FLAKA USES LIFE INSURANCE TO BUILD WEALTH

So if you put the $50,000 inside an insurance policy, from day one, that $50,000 immediately becomes $100,000. So if something happened to grandma the next day, next month, next year, or next decade, that money converts into a $100,000 income tax-free benefit to the named beneficiary.

When you're building wealth, a legacy, or creating generational wealth, make sure you have a solid foundation on which you can build. This will ensure that no matter what happens, you can continue your game plan for your family long into the future, regardless of any crisis or economic downturns.

While interviewed by DJ Akademiks, Waka Flocka said that when he was young, stupid, and unaware, he just blew his money. Recently, he put $2-3 million into a life insurance policy so he could let it grow. From there, he would have access to it. I did a reaction video to it and got over 250,000 views. That's a lot of views for a video talking about the life insurance game. None of my videos on my 7 Figure Squad YouTube channel has been promoted using any form of advertising—all organic traffic. People want to increase their financial awareness and take advantage of things they knew were there but were never exposed to. Check out the interview where he talks about how he uses life insurance to obtain wealth.

The United States of America has not experienced a bad market in the last fourteen years as it has from 2000 to 2010. Many people in the real estate, stock market, and crypto money game today have never experienced what a recession does to their plans. When it's bad, it's very bad, and no one can say when tough times end.

I've compared banks, the stock market, real estate, and life insurance. The answers speak for themselves, but I realize life insurance is not for everyone. Any home should be built on a solid foundation. I'm reminded of what the Good Book says in Matthew 7: 24-26 about the wise and foolish builder.

One builder built their home on the sand, and the other on a rock. It may seem to be faster or cost less to build on sand. There was less planning and more hoping that everything would be fine. When the weather is nice, and the waves are calm, it seems that you are in paradise. However, when the weather shifts, it comes with a great crash and washes away the home built on sand.

The wise builder who built on the rock chose to survey the land, devise a plan, and build with solid materials. Since he built upon a solid foundation, it withstood the beatings of the storm: no crash, no washing away, no starting all over again, no grief.

It is the same in building a financial home. You first have to start with a solid foundation that can provide answers, safety, and predictability during a crisis. Then, you want to make sure you put that foundation through many questions.

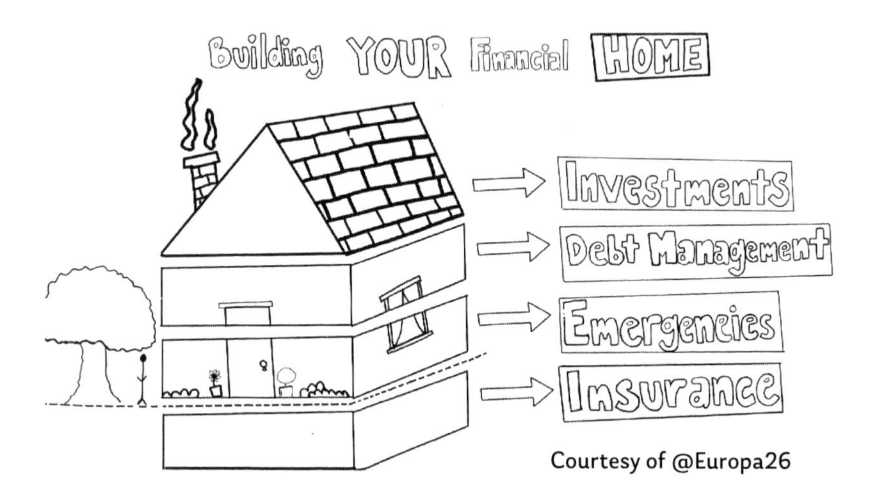

Courtesy of @Europa26

Let's talk about building your financial home. One of the most remarkable structures in the history of humankind is the pyramid, the triangle. At the bottom of the triangle, you want to establish a consistent, continual, secure cash flow.

Insurance

Remember, cash flow is king—because even the greatest financial strategy or plan will be destroyed if there's no cash flow to fund it. If you've been working hard and, sadly, you lose the ability to work and create cash flow due to an accident or unfortunate death, you'll end up unwinding everything you saved and invested to pay for expenses. This is where insurance provides the income tax-free resources to continue pushing forward your vision. People buy assets in the best of times. Insurance makes sure you keep them during the worst of times. You'll end up unwinding everything you saved and invested if you lack cash flow. People buy assets in the best of times. Insurance makes sure you keep them in the worst of times.

Emergencies

The next thing you want to establish is your savings or emergency fund. Savings is for when opportunities come up when uou or others are facing emergencies themselves. Your savings is your seed ready to plant or plug the gaps that create victorious situations out of tough times.

Debt-Management

Ask yourself, "How would I mitigate, minimize, or eliminate bad debt? Yes, that's right—you have to reduce bad debt. But, keep in mind—there's also good debt. Good debt means you can write off this interest based on the IRS tax code to acquire assets.

Good debt is if you're earning a return. If you're paying out at 3% in debt in order to earn 7%, you have a 4% profit. By the way, this is how banks make money using your money for their benefit by lending it out and earning interest above what they pay you. Do you understand why CDs, money market, and savings account interest are so low?

Investments

Here's where you can confidently go after building your stock and real estate portfolio, starting your own business, and getting more adventurous putting your money towards things for potential gain.

Sadly, this is where most people start and build their financial homes upside down. They get attracted to shiny new investment opportunities or find ways to retire sooner than later by taking unnecessary risks.

Many right away will go for the crypto, real estate, 401k, and then BAM—they lose their job or stumble into a reversal of fortune. Or you're in business, and you have either one client, vendor, or provider of material, and the next thing you know, they're not providing it anymore. Your whole financial vision is based on this one developing area of your financial home that stands the most risk to losing.

The best plans and investments can be washed away because you didn't build on it on a solid foundation. You chased the dollar instead of building your financial home on values and principles that have stood the test of time in the word of times.

Since money is something you will always need, it's vital that you make plans as early as possible to ensure you will always have enough. Sometimes, you'll need lots of money to accomplish major goals—like buying a home or starting a business. To make sure you have enough money to do these things, you should set clear financial goals and work towards achieving financial freedom.

PILLAR III

FITNESS & FUN

"Allow yourself to enjoy each happy moment in your life."

— Steve Maraboli

9

Holy Health and Wellness

"Health is like money, we never have a true idea of its value until we lose it."

—**Josh Billings**

Health is your first wealth. After playing sports growing up and serving eight years in the Marines, I can definitely appreciate a pain-free day! People often think about health and wellness in terms of physical health—nutrition, exercise, weight management, etc., but it is so much more. Wellness is a holistic integration of spiritual, mental, emotional, physical, and financial health. It is about fueling the body, engaging the mind, nurturing the spirit, and being aware of your finances.

Making the right choices for health and well-being can be challenging. Although we know what is good for us and how to do it and be better, we may not act on it. If we do, we may, in due time, slide back to familiar ways.

Human behavior—what we do, how we do it, and whether we will succeed— is significantly influenced by our habits. As Duhigg, author of *The Power of Habit: Why We Do What We Do in Life, and Business*, says, "Any behavior that can be reduced to a routine is one less behavior that we must spend time and energy consciously thinking about and deciding upon."

Habits are powerful. With about 40% of our everyday behavior repeated in the form of habits, they shape our very existence and, ultimately, our future.[13] They are the key to health. For better or worse, habits influence our well-being and quality of life. So if you are striving to improve these, you need to think about habits, because if you change your habits for the better, you change your life for the better. Sounds simple, right?

I was at the peak of my fitness when I left the Marines; however, it didn't take long for life to catch up to me. By my late 20s and all of my 30s, I took my health for granted. I'd work long hours and eat sporadically—with the majority of it being fast food or unhealthy choices. Next thing you know, I hit a wall. I realized I needed to make some significant changes in my health.

Before I knew it, I sounded like a Rice Krispies commercial when I got out of bed. Every joint in my body was like *snap, crackle, pop.* In my youth, I could easily reach down to pick something off the ground with ease. Later on, after serving in the Marines, bending down comes with a decision-making process of at least fifteen seconds of how I'm actually going to do that.

[13]Rubin G. Better Than Before: Mastering the Habits of Our Everyday Lives. Toronto, Ontario: Penguin Random House, Doubleday Canada; 2015.

As you age, if you go pick up a pencil that falls off your desk, if you aren't careful, you can strain your back, and you'll be down for a week. If you compete with the young guys at the office or gym, you could pull a hamstring or tear an Achilles tendon. Yes, this has happened.

Change became more achievable for me because I chose strategies that enhanced my chance for success. Such strategies include monitoring, scheduling, investing in systems of accountability, abstaining, and planning.

In a previous chapter, we discussed the different ways to create generational wealth. With that being said, it doesn't make sense to spend your entire life creating wealth and spend the rest of your life at the expense of regaining your health. But, unfortunately, it almost happened to me.

In my mid-forties, I started improving my health because I was in bad shape. I neglected my health in pursuit of financial stability, thinking that once my money was right, I could see the right doctors. Health, like wealth, erodes over time, especially if you aren't paying attention to it. Minor problems become costlier problems. I thought that "as a man," I could just suck it up, chew on some Motrin, and ignore the warning signs, and somehow, it would just take care of itself.

Automobiles often have red warning lights that signal us when something we cannot see is malfunctioning. Likewise, God has wonderfully designed our bodies so that they, too, signal us when they need special attention. Consistent dizziness, nausea, and pain in a specific area of the body are all examples of the danger signals that God allows our bodies to give us.

Sometimes, when a danger signal occurs, you may be aware of a possible cause. For example, if you feel sluggish, you should try getting to bed earlier. However, if your efforts don't help and the danger signal persists, you should consult a doctor.

After all, you would do at least as much for your car by taking it to a mechanic if it malfunctioned in some way! I had already ignored two torn patella tendons I got when I was in the military. I chose not to have surgery because I didn't want to be in a cast for six months. At that time, I couldn't afford to miss work and do what I needed to provide for my family.

Let's just say it was only a matter of time before I started breaking down. I ignored the check engine light and continued to work on other things until I experienced a kidney stone and thought my appendix had ruptured. The pain was excruciating.

I was constantly in pain with gout and arthritis. Calcium deposits formed all over my body because I refused to take medication. I had to stretch five minutes before getting out of bed. The cold weather made my body ache and feel so brittle that it took everything in my body to keep going.

I refused to listen to my body. I believed I could barrel through it. Then, when my youngest son was born, I remember making a promise that I would finally get healthy. I felt this kid would give me a run for my money—sure enough, he is the most rambunctious, energetic, fun-filled kid of the five. If I don't take care of my body, I would not be able to take care of him.

A lot of distractions will come in your life because your body is telling you it can or cannot handle the load. So in order to prepare for the fulfillment of your goal, purpose, ministry, and finances, you must watch over your temple—aka your body.

Good healthy habits show up in the kitchen and end up in the gym. Appropriate rest and hydration are key. I was fortunate to invest in a trainer and dietitian. There are days I intermittent fast and don't eat until 2 pm. I reduce sugar at all costs. I still enjoy ice cream and cookies, but I refuse to indulge regularly because I know the consequences of those choices. Cancer thrives in an acidic bodily environment which sugar helps create, so I know I can't eat much of it.

I had to take time to learn my body. In the Filipino culture, we eat rice with everything. And I mean *everything*. When I started understanding the effect food had on me, rice made me very lethargic in the afternoon. I had to make adjustments and understand my body. If I want to eat a lot during the day, it needs to consist mainly of protein and vegetables to keep me light and my mind sharp and clear. I'd eat my carbs at night, which improved my sleep. Maintaining a proper diet and exercise regimen is one of the greatest gifts you can do in following your faith–a gift that the Big Man upstairs places high value on.

High financial stress is twice as likely to report poor overall health.[14] Your financial, mental, and physical stress all correlate. Poor health can worsen money challenges and financial stress by increasing medical expenses. You can't go to work. You're not as productive at work, and making good financial and medical decisions is harder. With the way the medical system is in America, it's not cheap. Some people view quality medical care in America as a privilege. It's more about positioning yourself.

PHYSICAL AND FINANCIAL HEALTH

If there's one thing I've learned about my physical well-being over the years, it's this: There are no shortcuts, fad diets that will make me feel better, or innovative workouts that magically transform my body. Instead, it's all about persistence, planning, and a long-term commitment to constantly recreating myself.

I've seen many parallels between that and physical well-being. Of course, it takes time to produce significant results. But when you observe the full impact of all the little changes, it fuels you to keep putting in the work. The same applies to your bank account.

Education Powers Decision-Making

One thing most health and wellness professionals will tell you is to start tracking what you eat. As part of that process, you also may carefully read food labels. Why? Because we all need to get smarter about the food we put in our bodies. It is the fuel that drives us daily. Even that simple piece of education can go

[14]Keller, Abiola, University of Wisconsin - Madison, Does the Perception that Stress Affects Health Matter? The Association with Health and Mortality

a long way toward powering decisions about what we eat and, in turn, how healthy we can become. In order to make good decisions, we need to have good information.

Education is key to financial goals as well. You'll learn how to understand data and what trends it exposes. Getting out of debt doesn't have to be taxing (pun intended). Most often, we just don't know how to escape from it. Simple education can go a long way toward financial decision-making.

Long-Term Planning is the Key

Building endurance, both physically and financially, takes time. Strengthening muscles requires consistent effort. So does weight loss. Having a clear plan of attack is absolutely paramount to success. This is why personal trainers exist! I also enjoy having a trainer because going to the gym is the only time I don't have to make decisions.

You need a plan for your finances, just like you need that diet and exercise plan to stay physically healthy. Many could start by implementing a simple budget. Tracking spending each month, formulating a plan for how, where to spend your money, and how to save your money are great first steps. When you make small improvements daily, it will lead to a considerable improvement a year from now.

Remember the 50-30-20 Rule? A solid financial plan also makes the process less overwhelming. Instead of trying to do it all, it's broken out into approachable and realistic steps based on your specific situation and goals.

Practice Discipline

Physical well-being requires immense discipline. Intentionality comes with discipline. Do you eat to live or live to eat? Just like you have to have discipline with your financial decisions and discipline in your faith and prayer life, you should also have that discipline with food. When it comes to an over-indulgence, you must be aware of how much sweets you put in your body. It's hidden in everything!

There are always temptations—that piece of German chocolate cake, ice cream, or that cheeseburger you've been craving. But, with an actionable plan, an enjoyable process, and a better understanding of your physical health, it becomes easier to say no to that chocolate brownie or fast food visit.

With financial well-being, discipline is an absolute must. By being intentional and disciplined about spending and saving, you commit to your financial future. For example, I've often FaceTime'ed my trainer when I go to a restaurant so he can see the menu and recommend what I should eat. Straying from the plan is breaking a promise to yourself. The key is staying true to the process and knowing it might get arduous, but that is a part of it.

Many of the lessons and best practices people have learned when managing their physical health can also be applied to organizing their financial health.

I get another gear when it comes to business. I get another gear when it comes to my kids. I get another gear when it comes to travel. But then, there's jet lag, different time zones, and rushing to get to the right terminal—checking in, checking out, getting a rental car, and going to the hotel.

Then once you get to the hotel, you have meetings. After all that, you just want to lay down. Yet, you still need to keep the promise you made to yourself. So what's the easier thing to do? You're out and traveling; nobody's watching; you're away from your family and the office. Who's watching? That's when your purpose fuels you and discipline drives you.

Flexibility

Because of the scar tissue in my knees, I was stiff. Since my lower back kept cramping up, my chiropractor recommended an MRI; I discovered I had stenosis, the narrowing of my spinal column putting pressure on the nerves that go to my muscles. I felt like the Tin Man on Wizard of Oz, and I was only in my late 30s at this point. What was happening? I was suffering the consequences of failing to take care of my body. I took no supplements and ate the wrong foods. Now that I've got that squared away, it's an entirely different story.

When I finally went back to the gym just a couple of years ago, I could not jump on a six-inch platform. My trainer questioned why I wouldn't jump, I realized I had lost all trust in my body. I went from dunking in high school from a standing position below the rim to not being able to jump over a puddle.

Being in the insurance business, we're in a sedentary type of work. So when you combine lousy health with sedentary work, and you're on the computer a lot, when you're not on the computer, you're watching something on YouTube or Netflix, these behaviors worsen your health.

Benefits of physical and financial flexibility include:

- One provides freedom, and the other improves movement.
- One increases rest, and the other improves relaxation.
- One releases tension, and the other reduces soreness.
- One reduces risks, and the other reduces injury.

You will experience pain when you aren't stretched. Read that again. I'm not just talking about your body. If you don't stretch your mind, resources, and skills, you will continue to experience the pain of being average. It's better to do it sooner rather than later.

Many people are overlooked by the financial services industry when they need life insurance because they are ignorant about taking care of their bodies and the effects of diabetes, obesity, and high cholesterol. As a result, they get denied from using an essential financial tool.

I truly believe if we aren't taking care of our bodies, we won't be equipped to do what God has called us to do. The last thing I want God to do is to give my assignment to someone else because I was too irresponsible with my health and money. I want to be a warrior for God and those in our faith, fighting the good fight.

One of the main reasons why people file for bankruptcy is not because people charge up their credit cards or run out of money. Instead, the number one cause of bankruptcies is medical bills.

If aging parents need help around the house and their children are busy growing their careers or business and taking care of their own children, they won't be able to care for them the way they need. As a result, they have to depend on the United States government, local state, church, or charity for financial assistance. Is this what you want the people you love and care about to do? Is this what you feel that your faith has led you to accomplish? Unfortunately, being in the insurance industry, I often see the ill combination of financial and health sickness on a daily basis.

MENTAL AND EMOTIONAL HEALTH

Mental health includes emotional, psychological, and social well-being. It affects how we think, feel, act, and relate to others. It's more than the absence of a mental illness—it's essential to your overall health and quality of life.

Emotionally healthy people are in control of their thoughts, feelings, and behaviors. They're able to cope with life's challenges. They can keep problems in perspective and bounce back from setbacks. They feel good about themselves and have good relationships.

Being mentally healthy doesn't mean you're happy all the time. It means you're aware of your emotions. You can deal with them, whether they're positive or negative. Emotionally healthy people still feel stress, anger, and sadness, but they know how to manage their negative feelings. They can tell when a problem is more than they can handle on their own.

Not taking care of your physical body and mental health have numerous adverse effects. Some of the ones that have the greatest impact are the following:

Brain Fog

Your decision-making is affected when you aren't able to think clearly due to the foods you are putting in your body. It can also create other health problems associated with not caring for yourself. You're more susceptible to making bad decisions if you're not mentally sharp.

Recovery

I've seen a lot of good, hard-working people put in tons of time and effort. I believe in hard work, just like anybody else. I believe in putting in the long hours necessary to do the emotional lifting of building your dream. However, if they don't take care of their body throughout that process and allow it to recover, their effectiveness is cut too short.

The wealth accumulation, ministry, innovation, or impact was cut too short. When I interviewed Tim Grover, personal trainer to Dwayne Wade and Michael Jordan, he told me about having to tell Kobe to sleep when he refused to. He told Kobe that sleeping was training, so he didn't think he wasn't putting in work.

Burnout

We're all human, and we all have our moments of frustration, but if you consistently feel irritable and anxious, it's a sign that you're too burned out to handle the many small annoyances life throws at you.

When our physical or mental health suffers, it's a no-brainer that we'll feel on edge and easily annoyed. However, if you find yourself constantly getting angry or upset over things you know are irrational, it's time to pivot. There's almost always a reason, whether physical or mental—and taking care of it can help you begin to feel better.

We can talk about financial education all you like, but if your body and mental state fail to handle pressure and stress, you won't endure trials for long.

FOUR ENEMIES OF GREATNESS

Everyone has vices or things that get them sidetracked. We've all been there—the key is to leave as soon as you arrive. In his bestselling book, *Your Next Five Moves*, Patrick Bet-David shares what he learned from Pastor Dudley Rutherford when it comes to 4G's—and I'm not ιalking about your wireless plan.

The four enemies of greatness are:

1. Greed
2. Gambling
3. Gluttony
4. Girls/Guys

Greed: It is not difficult to fall into the trap of greed. Ambition, setting goals, and having dreams is great, but if you feel you have to win by stabbing someone in the back or taking from someone else, you don't deserve it. Greed will have you chasing money instead of attracting it.

Gambling: Gambling taps into the lazy side of human nature. People are gambling with crypto—with all of their investments. They end up having nothing to show for it. You're mistaken if you think you will get rich without doing the work. Even if you did get some money, the likelihood of you keeping it is slim to none. The only way I "gamble" is if I know the odds and whether or not I control them—which really isn't much of a gamble.

Gluttony: Gluttony is the excessive consumption that deprives another being of a life-giving necessity. Gluttons devour more, leaving others with less. It's immoderation. Beyond consumption, gluttony is the worship of food and its excessive pleasure. It also extends into material goods and other physical pleasures. The suffix "-aholic" (workaholic, shopaholic) is attached to the glutton's "meal" of choice.

Girls/guys: You get easily distracted by someone of the opposite sex. If it ends up being a toxic relationship, you will find yourself far off the beaten path of where you started. I can't tell you how many wrong relationships people have gotten into because of physical attraction. I'll share more about sexual temptation and God's perspective in the next chapter regarding this topic.

I could have easily let any of these things keep me from greatness. I think back to my high school years at the horse tracks. I felt the surge of instant gratification, and the enemy used gambling to try and take me out. I continued betting and winning, betting and losing until I hit rock bottom.

It could have easily become an addiction. I believe that's why I refuse to gamble now because most of the time, I give up something and receive nothing in return. External pleasures had me cutting corners. I ended up broke right before committing to the Marines. It's easy for one of these to lead to the other; eventually, you'll find yourself far off the beaten track. The only way I could overcome this is by getting with the right people willing to pull me aside to help me make better decisions because distractions are going to be there.

BIRTH OF AN ENTREP-ATHLETE

As a kid, I wanted to be a pro-athlete. However, my body, DNA, and skill set were far from what was necessary to rise beyond the high school level. For this reason, I was never an all-conference prep athlete, all-state, or an all-American.

However, I admire how athletes prepare and approach their craft and, of course, the money and experience they get to live. Becoming an entrepreneur was the closest thing I could do to that feel of high-level competition, recognition, and income level. I wanted to treat business like pro athletes treat their sport. Hence the birth of the #EntrepAthlete!

Any poor habits I create with my health will spill into my family and work life unless I consciously attempt to change them. On the flip side, the habits I create do the same. For example, treating people with kindness and empathy is just as beneficial in my personal life as it is in my professional life. Both of them attribute to my leadership abilities.

Once I realized that my lofty goals and dreams of one day being a professional athlete were gone when I enlisted in the military. However, I still carried the desire to be somebody, to be respected, and to bring honor to my family name. Years later, I realized I could make some professional athlete income in the insurance industry. But, I wouldn't ever have to take the game field, put on shoulder pads, or strap up.

So once I started a business, I adopted the mantra of taking what was instilled in me from my faith, family, sports, and military and creating a business. My philosophy of treating business like a professional athlete treats his sport started to manifest on our platform in the insurance industry.

Review the Play

An athlete reviews their film the same way I would review my financial statements in a presentation and during a one-on-one conversation with a client. I took notes during board meetings to critique my technique. So the next time I went into the board room to meet with a client, I would approach it from a different angle.

Whenever a new opportunity came my way, I could see better results because I reviewed and learned from the last opportunity. It's one thing to make the appointment, and it's another thing to debrief from it and learn how to enhance your system.

This self-analyzation process takes energy and time. Thankfully, I don't have to take a beating on the field as these pro-athletes do but being an entrepreneur does take a substantial mental beating. The mental beating will be magnified if your physical body is not ready for it.

Train Your Body

People in the bodybuilding and fitness world put their bodies through strict diets. It's one of the most disciplined sports I've come to recognize. They cut out carbs, weigh their food, and meal-prep for the entire week. They also take vitamins and supplements to enhance their health.

If you look at how a bodybuilder competes from an entrepreneurial lens, they can do that with their body with diet and exercise to maximize their health at the optimal level. The same transferrable skills, values, and principles can be used in business.

The Bible says, "Everyone who competes in the games goes into strict training. They do it to get a crown that will not last, but we do it to get a crown that will last forever." (1 Corinthians 9:25).

Athletes get in shape so that they can achieve an award. As an entrepreneur, I want every part of my life to be in shape to achieve success and receive an eternal price. I've quickly embraced that the ultimate reward is making the most of what I've been given and caring for my body so God can use me more effectively.

Create Routine

Look at Kobe Bryant, for example. He would get up at 4:00 in the morning, work out in the gym from 5:00 to 7:00 am, come back home for breakfast, and drop the kids off at school. Then he had another workout from 9:00 to 11:00 am. Next, he ate lunch, then worked out again from 2:00 to 4:00 pm. Finally, he had dinner and was back at the gym from 7:00 to 9:00 pm. He was doing four-a-days. The compound effect of that regimented schedule created a separation between him and other players in the league. They just couldn't keep up.

Even though Kobe wasn't the strongest, fastest, tallest, quickest player in the entire league, he recognized that. However, he did the most with whatever God-given skill set he had. As a result, he was one of the greatest of all time. He embodied the Mamba Mentality and refused to settle.

It's all about conditioning. When it's time to make the play, it's easier because I've been working out. I'm more prepared. My body is equipped with the ability it needs to perform. Not only did I do basic training in the military, but I've also done basic training in life so I can handle the unexpected things that come my way. Seeking God is another way I've been able to make tough decisions that have been detrimental to how I live.

I'm not telling you to start working out four times a day, but there needs to be an urgency to get in shape where you're not winded or carrying unnecessary weight.

Our world witnessed what happens when people with pre-existing conditions get hit with certain illnesses. The biggest problem with COVID wasn't necessarily the virus; it exposed people's health prior to getting sick. While I am sensitive to those who lost loved ones, the majority of people who were severely impacted had underlining health issues, including COPD, obesity, and other illnesses that directly affected the lungs.

It is natural for all of us to desire physical health with a body that is free of disease and functioning at its best. However, if you desire to improve your chances of enjoying the best that life offers, instead of just a financial component, consider investing in every area of your health—including your spiritual health.

I was telling my trainer about pain in my lower back. Instead of adjusting my back, he said he needed to adjust my hamstrings and release my tight hips and psoas muscle.

I asked, "What are you talking about? Why do you need to adjust my hamstrings? I told you my lower back was tight."

As he started loosening my hamstrings and hips, he responded, "No, man, everything is connected."

Miraculously enough, my back started feeling better. The area you think needs to be adjusted might not be the area that relieves you of pain. It could be the areas surrounding it that are causing tension. That's when I replayed his words in my mind—everything is connected. And it is. Our bodies are all connected. All aspects of our health and lives are connected: spiritually, mentally, physically and emotionally.

In the next chapter, I want to dive into what honoring your body looks like from a biblical perspective. It is great to treat your body well—eat right, challenge your body, get proper sleep—because you'll be rewarded with more energy, greater focus, and a heightened level of discipline. You'll achieve new levels of productivity while your competition falls behind and watches you scale faster and faster.

Implementing a healthy lifestyle is imperious to transform you into a world-class entrepreneur or business owner and stack more money in your bank account. There are a lot of aspects of your spiritual health that can improve things with your physical, mental, emotional, and financial health.

Everything discussed in this chapter is the key to the success of today's most influential entrepreneurs, artists, experts, thought leaders, industry titans, and anyone else who performs at a high level. I believe it is also God's desire to take care of ourselves; this was undoubtedly part of His plan for us as we see it in the Garden of Eden.

In 3 John chapter two, the following prayer is offered: "Dear friend, I pray that you may enjoy good health and that all may go well with you, even as your soul is getting along well." And in John 10:10, Christ says, " ... I have come that they may have life, and have it to the full." The full includes our mental, emotional, physical, and financial health, but our spiritual health and relationship with the Creator are the driving force of our purpose.

10

Honor Your Temple

"Take care of your body.
It's the only place you have to live in."

—Jim Rohn

In 1 Corinthians 6:19-20, the Bible says, "Do you not know that your bodies are temples of the Holy Spirit, who is in you, whom you have received from God? You are not your own; you were bought at a price. Therefore, honor God with your bodies." This is one of the most popular verses, but it is often misinterpreted. What does it mean? Why does temple imagery fit well with the bodies God has designed for us? How can we treat our bodies like a temple?

The Holy Spirit indwells our bodies; therefore, we need to take care of our bodies. Our physicality relates directly to what we typically think of as our spiritual well-being. Through our bodies, we do God's will in the world. Our body and spirit are connected, integrated, and united. What happens to one affects the other. How aware are you that your bodily experiences are integral to your spiritual life?

In his letter, Paul rebukes the church for an array of issues. Evidently, the church in Corinth was struggling with their sexual purity because that is what this verse is directly addressing. Paul implores us to recognize that our bodies are not our own but belong to God. Because we have been bought at a price (1 Corinthians 7:23) by Jesus Christ's death and resurrection, as stated in, we don't have any right to give them over to sin.

Some people have the wrong attitude toward your body. We neglect and reject it ("God, I want a different one!"), or we try to perfect it (the way some bodybuilders might worship their bodies). Instead, God wants us to respect our body and protect it. Why? Because God created it, Jesus paid for it, and the Holy Spirit lives in it.

When we look at our bodies—where the Holy Spirit, our energy, purpose, and calling dwells (whatever that definition is for you), you have to learn how to be of service to yourself. While staying faithful to my relationship with God, I first began to face my profound ambivalence about life in a body. I could no longer ignore the fact that I was tired and lethargic.

As I mentioned in the previous chapter, I started looking closely at my physical condition: eating patterns, water intake, how much sleep I was getting, whether I was exercising, and general attention to health issues. However, although I was paying attention to my spiritual life for years, I ignored the connection between my physical well-being and my life following my faith.

It reminds me of the story of Elijah's journey into God's presence in 1 Kings 19. I was struck by the attention God gave to Elijah's physical condition, going so far as to send an angel to guide him in caring for his body. I was comforted that even though Elijah was a great prophet, he had the same blind spot I seemed to have. He had let himself become so run down physically that God had to send an angel to strengthen his body before they could deal with anything else. The angel got very specific with Elijah providing him with a cake baked on hot stones (the first angel food cake, I presume) and a jar of water.

Elijah followed the angel's simple instructions and then fell into such an exhausted sleep that he almost slept through the next meal. The angel came a second time, touched him, and said, "Get up and eat, otherwise, the journey will be too much for you."

"What journey?" Elijah might have asked. After all, he had left his life as a prophet in Israel; he had slumped down under a solitary broom tree and told God in uncertain terms that he was done. But the angel knew better. He knew that Elijah was on a deeper spiritual journey—the journey into the presence of God. And *that* journey requires strength of both body and soul.

Ephesians 2:10 tell us we are God's masterpiece, created to do the good things that He had planned a long time ago for us to do. The more fit and healthy we are, the more energy we will have. The more energy we have, the more we can put into whatever task we do.

If you're not active or keeping your health in check, you limit your ability to follow your faith, bring honor to your Creator, and contribute to a more significant cause. Proverbs 14:30 says, "A heart at peace is life to the body." When you're not physically well, it only dominoes into more problems, creating separation from Him.

Our mental alertness is affected by our diet and activity, so the less attention you give to your physical well-being, the less attention you can give to the people who matter most in your life. When we see the health of our parents, children, and even friends declining, we often do everything in our power to challenge them to live healthier lives. We must do the same for ourselves.

God's commandments concerning our physical health are for our own spiritual good. Proverbs 3:1-2 says, "My son, do not forget my teaching but let your heart keep my commandments, for the length of days and years of life and peace they will add to you." He promises to bless us physically and spiritually if we honor what the Lord commands in our hearts.

Before I continue with the external portion of our bodies, I would be remiss if I did not share about prayer and meditation as the primary focus of honoring God. After all, it is through the time of listening and speaking to God that you can see how to improve your health.

PRAYER AND MEDITATION

Prayer is talking to God. Meditation is *listening* to God. For most people, life is frequently fast-paced and stressful. Everyone needs time to sit back and gain perspective on what they are here for and how they conduct themselves in their daily lives. This reflection and introspection—looking inside oneself—can be done through prayer and meditation.

You may pray frequently, or you may never have prayed. If you don't believe in prayer, give it a shot. It's the beginning of a relationship your Creator wants to establish with you.

You will begin to grow spiritually when you operate according to spiritual principles. Whether or not you fully believe in the power of prayer does not matter right now. The important thing is to train your mind to be open to prayer and meditation. You have nothing to lose and everything to gain.

Meditation aims to clear your mind of racing thoughts, center yourself, and let go of fears, jealousy, blame, and control. When you meditate, you will learn to listen. Whenever your mind is racing with too many stressful thoughts of what you should be doing, what needs to be done, and what you should have done two weeks ago, focus on your breathing and make a conscious attempt to slow down and take full, long breaths.

Soon, you'll be able to use deep breathing to clear your mind for several minutes, eventually even longer. Then, when obsessive, stressful thoughts catch up with you, refocus your breathing.

Keep practicing this, regardless of how often it takes before you see concrete results.

To maintain God's peace, we must give up the need to be right, along with the need to be in control. Instead, we must humble ourselves and give it all to God, trusting that we will be shown the way to whatever it is we need to know and who is in control.

Peace must come from within us before we can help bring it to anyone else. Peace does not come from outside us, even if we travel across the world searching for it; we will not find it anywhere but inside ourselves, as it is already within us, just where it has always been.

I discovered that some spiritual practices coincided quite naturally with my physical disciplines. For example, times of working out became moments of turning my heart toward God. I found myself naturally using those times to connect with God. While my body was occupied with physical activity, my heart and mind were freed up to reflect on my day and invite God to help me notice those times when the Spirit was at work guiding, protecting, and comforting me. There have been a few times my trainer noticed I had an unusual burst of energy and had to come down from my spiritual high with tears flowing during a challenging set.

FASTING

Fasting is the most concrete and viscerally embodied of the spiritual disciplines. It also intersects the physical and the metaphysical and produces uniquely potent effects that bridge the gap between body and soul.

In recent times, fasting has become popular for its health effects alone, but when also practiced as a spiritual discipline, it can unlock far more possibilities than can be read on a scale. The constant craving for pleasure can be detrimental, and occasional discomfort can be necessary to experience a breakthrough.

Fasting is an intimate experience I've incorporated into my life over the last ten years. During my fasting, I am more creative, strategic, and expansive.

In Luke 4:4, one of Satan's challenges to Jesus was turning a stone into bread after Jesus had fasted forty days and nights. Jesus answered him, "It is written, 'Man shall not live by bread alone.'" He was referring to the words in the Old Testament, "He humbled you, causing you to hunger and then feeding you with manna, which neither you nor your ancestors had known, to teach you that man does not live on bread alone but on every word that comes from the mouth of the Lord" (Deuteronomy 8:3, NIV).

There are several types of Christian fasting: Partial Fasting, The Daniel Fast, Complete Fasting, Absolute Fasting, Sexual Fasting, Corporate Fasting, and a Soul Fast.[15]

The fasts should be done with an attitude of humility and a hunger for deepening your faith and distancing us from fears. When denying ourselves, we set aside the time we would be

---

[15]Julia Oates, Just Disciple, Types of Fasting & Whats Right for You

eating to pray, read the Bible, and honor our Maker.

I fast because it is easy to get caught up in the now and forget Who is in control. When money isn't an issue, ego can try to take over, thinking that your progress was all you. Fasting provides concrete, visceral practice in choosing higher principles over lower appetites.

In feeling physical hunger but disregarding its pull, you teach yourself that you're the boss of your body and God is in control. For example, one of the first fasts I did was fasting from meat. As a result, I had pains and withdrawals by creating a different eating pattern, but God sustained my hunger.

After fasting, I have experienced breakthroughs in relationships and business. When I thought something would happen one way, God revealed that it would occur differently. There were two instances when there were opportunities I had no way of foreseeing that happened. If you haven't ever fasted, I encourage you to do your research to see if it's something you are led to do.

What do you do when you are alone with your fork and spoon? In Philippians 3:19, overeating and other overindulgence are bad things because they set up food and other earthly pleasures as gods, which we worship. In 1 Corinthians 9:24-27, we see the principles of keeping our bodily desires under control for a more critical objective.

Whatever you feel led to do or what your calling is, you will not be able to get there if your body does not follow. You will be able to get there if you sacrifice the ability for you to move. To be good stewards of our bodies, we must do our best to have a healthy weight in proportion to our height and bone structure.

I'm not trying to be an Instagram model. I want to be confident and have the capacity to be able to serve and contribute for as long as possible. We can all strive to eat in moderation to stay healthy and prevent food from becoming an idol in our lives.

Whatever strengthens my spirit inside weakens my first emotional impulses and decisions. When I strengthen my spiritual relationship with God, I mature in my emotional and financial arenas. It spills over in areas I never expected.

In our modern world, fasting has become a huge health craze, but when the Spirit of God leads a believer to fast, it has more than just health benefits and a diet. It has spiritual benefits that can transform us. A spiritual fast is when we abstain from food or a select type of food (like a Daniel Fast) to draw closer to the Lord. The word fast in Hebrew actually means to shut the mouth or cover the mouth.

Usually, the times when one would be eating would be replaced with time praying and seeking the Lord. This is why you always see the terms prayer and fasting. They go together.

I want to point out that some consider removing other things from their life as fast. An example would be fasting on social media or watching TV. However, these types of fasting are not in Scripture. And some debate if this is truly a form of Biblical fasting since the Hebrew is clear it is about covering the mouth, pertaining to food.

But if you feel led by the Lord to remove something from your life, I encourage you to follow that nudge. Sometimes, when you remove time suckers, you'll find you have much more time to spend with the Lord.

The thing is that when we spiritually fast, we should not shout about it but quietly seek the Lord in our prayer closets, knowing that He is the only one who needs to hear our prayers. When I am fasting, I do not broadcast it to everyone. No one needs a special pat on the back or recognition from others that they are strengthening their faith and relationship with their Creator.

Fasting makes us sensitive to the voice of God because we remove our focus from food. When we fast, we set our minds on things of the spirit and avoid things of the flesh. Therefore, we hear God more clearly when we don't have the distraction of food on our minds.

God has a lot to say to us, and when we fast, we are more in tune with what He desires for us.

Determination to Resist Temptation

Fasting strengthens our spirits to resist temptation because we focus on feeding our spirits. Sometimes we get caught up in seasons where we give in to the flesh's desires or feel extremely tempted. A fast gives us the reset we need to continue to grow in our faith and resist the devil (James 4:7).

Jesus says, "Watch and pray, lest you enter into temptation. The spirit indeed is willing, but the flesh is weak" (Matthew 26:41). Jesus recognized that the spirit is willing to walk away from temptation, but the flesh has trouble doing so. How often have you known the right thing to do and did the opposite? Fasting strengthens our spirits to resist temptation and keep away from regretful decisions.

Deliverance and Discernment

God delivers us from the spiritual bondage that holds us back when we fast. He frees us from influences and different things that keep us bound in life. Isaiah 58:6 states, "Is this not the fast that I have chosen: To loose the bonds of wickedness, To undo the heavy burdens, To let the oppressed go free, And that you break every yoke?"

God gives us a way out of difficult situations when we seek Him through fasting and prayer. This means we always have victory over the enemy and all the devices he uses against us.

Detox the Body and Soul

When we fast, we clear our souls and bodies from impurities that hinder our progress. In addition, our bodies benefit from fasting because they get to release a buildup of toxins that we ingest daily.

Daniel and his three friends refused the food and wine from the king because they believed the food would defile them. Daniel 1:15 says, "And at the end of ten days, their features appeared better and fatter in flesh than all the young men who ate the portion of the king's delicacies." After Daniel determines in his heart not to eat the food, the Lord favors Daniel and his fellow captives so that the guard accepts the alternate plan for a trial period. God was active in preserving Daniel and his friends—they might very well have been executed for their refusal of the king's direct order!

Our bodies also benefit by cutting out food for a period of time to seek God. We also give our souls a much-needed cleanse because we focus on God and His mighty power, not our problems or challenges.

Desire for Faith

Fasting gives us a new desire to follow our faith and strengthen our spiritual muscle. Where our faith begins to wane, God revives us and renews our passion for godly things. Spiritual hunger increases as we eat more spiritually. Colossians 3:2 says, "Set your mind on things above, not on things on the earth." Fasting helps us draw closer to our faith, igniting our passion for Him to lead our lives in a better way.

Sound eating habits benefit your physical health. That is probably one reason the Israelites were warned about eating the fat of animals (Leviticus 3:17). Daniel benefited from eating vegetables and water instead of rich food (Daniel 1:12-15). Each of us needs to prayerfully study what qualified nutritionists have to say concerning the food we eat, and then we should apply the advice to our diets. The following are some points that many experts recommend:

- Eat a balanced diet (natural foods): Candy and other highly processed snacks shouldn't make up a significant portion of your diet.
- Significantly reduce your refined sugar intake and reduce some of your meat consumption. Unfortunately, most Americans consume far too much sugar and probably too much meat for optimum health.
- Eat your food closer to the state where God created it rather than in a highly altered form. For example, raw or lightly cooked vegetables are generally superior in nutritional value to highly cooked or processed vegetables.
- Eliminate beverages that contain caffeine or alcohol from your diet. Instead, you can drink several healthy alternatives, such as herbal tea, decaffeinated coffee, and grain-based beverages.

Before we ever begin pursuing our heart's desires, we must know they line up with God's Word and will. The more time you spend with God—seeking Him and obeying His Word—the more certain you will be that your heart's desires match His will. In fact, when you honor Him, He puts those desires in your heart (Psalm 37:4). They become in sync with His will.

WAYS TO HONOR GOD

Honoring God recognizes Him as the highest authority in heaven and on Earth. He is the One who created the universe, from the largest planet to the tiniest grain of sand, and no person, power, spirit, or force can contend with His greatness and might.

Another key revelation to honoring God is recognizing that we need a loving Savior's mercy, grace, and power to love, protect, and guide us on our life journey.

1. Sabbath

Psalm 127:2 says, "In vain you rise early and stay up late, toiling for food to eat—for he grants sleep to those he loves." In Mark 6:30-32, Jesus advises His disciples to take some special time just to rest.

What about you? Are you "toiling for food to eat?" Do you need to take time out to rest?

People seem to vary regarding how much sleep they need at night. But whatever the right amount is for you, your health demands you get it. Generally speaking, it is better to go to bed at the same time each evening and wake up at the same time every morning. Your body will become accustomed to the schedule and will be ready to rest fully at the given time.

Hebrews four discusses the importance of rest and says God desires us to enter His rest. In addition to a good night's sleep, you may need to have a time during the day when you can take a break from whatever you've been working on, put your feet up, and just relax for a while. My Sabbath is from Saturday late evening to Sunday at 6:00 pm. That's when I recover and rejuvenate from the week. It is time dedicated to God and my family.

2. Self-Control

Don't allow the devil to grab a foothold (Ephesians 4:27). If your right eye causes you to sin, metaphorically pluck it out (Matthew 5:39).

Don't put yourself in an environment that puts you at a higher risk of engaging in the area where you are tempted to do the wrong thing. For example, if you have a history of alcoholism, don't schedule meetings at a bar. If you struggle with infidelity, stop going to clubs. If you struggle with drugs, stop hanging around people that do it.

Instead, redirect this energy into an area that builds you up or call someone that understands your journey. For example, I replaced going to clubs with building a business driven by hitting deadlines. I replaced a struggle with alcohol by asking friends or business partners to go to lunch, dinner, or hit the gym with me. I created positive distractions.

As I mentioned in chapter nine, many distractions can keep us from reaching our fullest potential. Avoid areas where you have a weakness. You have to emit self-control and minimize the distractions that take you away from seeking, serving, or fulfilling your purpose.

We all have times when we are tempted, but the key is not falling into the temptation and relying on God. I heard a story about a man who was trying to get healthy.

After deciding it was time to shed a few pounds, he visited a nutritionist, went on a new diet, started going to the gym, and took it seriously. He even changed his usual driving route to the office to avoid his favorite donut shop. Everyone he knew was cheering him on. He finally started making progress!

One morning, however, he arrived at the office carrying a large, chocolate Bavarian-creme-filled donut. His co-workers had perplexed expression written all of their faces, but he only smiled and shrugged his shoulders.

Breaking the silence, he said, "This is a very special donut. This morning, out of my forced habit, I accidentally drove by my favorite donut shop. I felt that it was no accident that I happened to pass by, so I went into prayer to fight the temptation."

He continued, "So I prayed, 'God if you really want me to have one of these delicious coffee cakes, you'll help me a parking spot right in front.' Sure enough, on the ninth trip around the block, there it was!"

Proverbs 25:28 says, "A man without self-control is like a city broken into and left without walls." Spiritual self-control cannot happen without strengthening your faith. You must depend on God's guidance and draw upon His power and strength;

our Creator has given us self-control and discipline. How we do one thing is how we'll do everything.

1 Corinthians 10:13 says, "No temptation has overtaken you except what is common to mankind. And God is faithful; he will not let you be tempted beyond what you can bear. But when you are tempted, he will also provide a way out so that you can endure it." If you never make your temptations obey, you won't be able to control your actions. If you're not willing to stop yourself, then you're not going to stop yourself from having an affair or doing something you'll regret that may have lasting consequences. It's endless.

3. Serve

When you honor your faith and God by serving, He will begin to touch the broken areas in your life and bring healing in ways you could never imagine. Serving consistently over a period of time will transform your life. It's so much more than one act; it's the relationships you gain, the love for the church you develop, your faith that you deepen, and the community you bond with.

We are all called to serve in some way; we honor God by fulfilling His good and perfect purpose for us through our service. Opportunities for growth as a Christian are always associated with serving alone or alongside others, helping others. It is simply people helping people.

God does not need our compliments. But, He knows we need to serve to be genuinely fulfilled. So, whether it be random acts of kindness or planned activities, we should keep our eyes and ears open, searching for opportunities to bless others. You will be blessed as you serve, and God will be honored.

CARE FOR YOUR PHYSICAL APPEARANCE

One of the characteristics God has given you is your physical appearance. However, consider the quality and beauty of the material and the skillfulness of workmanship that went into building God's temple in Solomon's time (1 Kings 5-7).

I know many people who have become lax in taking care of their appearance. As a result, they suffer from a tremendous lack of confidence and a corresponding depreciation in their ability to function well with others.

You can take care of your physical appearance and present yourself in the best way possible without becoming vain. This doesn't mean you need to have designer clothes and the most expensive shoes at all times, but you can think about how you look.

I remember one of the first things my drill instructor told us in boot camp as we learned how to iron our uniforms to prepare for inspection. He'd say, "If you look good, you feel good. You do good; that's all good." When I interviewed Deion "Primetime" Sanders, he said, "If you look good, you play good, and it pays good!"

People who are self-conscious about their appearance will find it more exhausting to step out and be bold and confident about the calling in their lives. Because we are God's masterpiece, we should honor and glorify Him in our appearance just as we would seek to in other areas.

Not to say this is right, but people will judge a book by its cover.

STRENGTH TO CONTINUE

Billy Graham continued serving God for decades because he stayed in shape. He took care of his body and brought so many souls to Christ. Now, as a man of wealth and power, what would have happened if he used serving God as an excuse not to prioritize his health. He wouldn't have been able to serve God to the magnitude he did.

Investing in your health by what you eat and working out for forty-five minutes to an hour improves productivity. It also honors God, which we will discuss in the next chapter.

It's imperative to start where you are. Start somewhere. If you go to the gym three to four times a week, you're ahead of who you used to be. The older you get, the more refined you become and the more you're able to avoid many of these health challenges and problems that may come if you weren't taking care of your health.

Having an environment conducive to where you want to be is indispensable. If you are around people who don't prioritize their health, you will be less likely to do the same. However, if you get around people who are peak performers, you'll realize you need to kick it in gear and step it up.

The progression is personal. If you start drinking water and working out instead of laying around eating Snickers and drinking soda all day, don't beat yourself up because you don't look like a professional athlete or cheerleader. It took years for them to get to where they are, just like it took years for your unhealthy habits to catch up to you. You must start the journey of improving and reversing the results of bad habits.

Spiritual disciplines help us know the difference between the excesses of a culture that glorifies and objectifies the body and religious traditions that have often denigrated and ignored the body.

Moments of physical activity and exercise become prayers of gratitude and moments of consecration. Likewise, eating healthy food that we enjoy can be an occasion of experiencing God's care for us, reminding us of our dependency on Him and His faithfulness to care for our needs.

God created us for wholeness. When aspects of ourselves meant to exist together are reintegrated, the result is a combustion of joy and vitality that goes far beyond the physical dimension. It is a *spiritual* vitality essential to the abundance of our life in faith.

11

Enjoy the Fruit of Your Labor

"You shall eat the fruit of the labor of your hands; you shall be blessed, and it shall be well with you."
— Psalm 128:2

Do you remember having fun as a child? It should not be a part of the past. I assure you, it's possible to have fun, even with many responsibilities. Learning to relax is an art; having fun in life is another.

One of the biggest reasons people can't seem to have fun in life is that they don't even know what brings them true joy. To live a meaningful life, you need to add fun and shake things up a bit.

Living life without fun can be very boring and also very unhealthy. I spent years not having fun, only to realize it was missing. I didn't want to work and pay bills. I didn't wish just to exist. I wanted to live and have fun doing it.

After six days of creation, God looked upon the works of his hands and pronounced them "very good" (Genesis 1:31). It is important to note that the sanctity of rest in no way undervalues the importance of work. Instead, work is an indispensable requirement for rest and enjoyment. God affirms the goodness of work and the sacredness of rest, with the two beautifully woven together.

Rest and recreation are so important that God put them in the "Big 10"—right up there with not committing adultery, murdering, and stealing. You'd say, "Well, I'd never murder anybody or commit adultery." But are you taking a day off every week? God didn't make a day of rest for *His* benefit. He made it for ours: "The Sabbath was made to benefit man, and not man to benefit the Sabbath" (Mark 2:2).

When I ignore God's laws, who gets hurt? Not God. Rest is law. I'd like to say fun is, too.

The opening chapters of Genesis establish a pattern of work and rest; to do one without the other is a deviation from God's created order. So God blessed them and said, "Be fruitful and increase in number; fill the earth and subdue it. Rule over the fish in the sea and the birds in the sky and over every living creature that moves on the ground" (Genesis 1:28).

It is very disheartening if you labor and another eats, you sow and another reaps, you gather money, and another eats it. But I'll save that discussion for another time or book since this is one of the last chapters! The Bible says you are to enjoy the fruit of the labor of *your* hands—which means you are responsible for putting in the work. Therefore, God instructs us to work.

When your labor yields monetary resources, you can use the money for your enjoyment—all while creating a life you enjoy and not one you have to escape. After years of investing as an entrepreneur in a successful business, then your goal may be taking your family to Monaco—or purchasing your dream car (which may or may not be a white Rolls-Royce Dawn). But, again, it's to be used for what *you* enjoy.

I was impacting and serving a greater purpose as a United States Marine. It was honorable, and I felt a deep sense of pride every time I would put on the uniform. However, I was financially miserable as I attempted to raise kids based on a military salary. My income was not sustaining my family's financial needs with hazardous duty pay.

I knew if I continued what I was doing, the grueling hours would catch up to me. I would go away on deployment to bring money in for my kids, whom I couldn't see because of all the jobs I was working—not including the time I spent away during deployment. I was risking my life to make a living for my kids, but our time together was limited. After calculating my time in the military, I earned a quarter-million dollars with nothing to show for it but everything to owe for it.

During the time I was working three jobs, I was scraping by to pay bills, but I learned a lot of excellent skills. For example, I learned how to earn tips for additional income as a bartender at Marine Corps Air Station El Toro Officers Club. In addition, I learned to cut hair. Then all my Marines would ask me for a high and tight on Friday mornings before the weekend started. If you haven't been able to tell, I had quite a few jobs before I started in insurance.

When I look back at my work week, being created in God's image, I want to say, "It is very good," the same thing God said when He looked back at His creation. The feeling of productiveness lets me know I made a difference at the end of each day. It gives me a sense of accomplishment.

Why do you work—or are you just working to pay bills? Do you enjoy your career? Can you see the fruit from where you spend most of your time? Unfortunately, my experience is that most people don't love their work. Many like it, some tolerate it, but only a minority find work they love that also supports their lifestyle.

I have counseled numerous people to find they are working their current jobs because they have food on the table and a roof over their heads. Life isn't not going to be luxurious all the time, but you can and should find enjoyment in your work. Doing so is very valuable to your life in many ways, including significantly increasing your probability of financial success. We all need to love life to benefit from it fully; the parts which generate that zeal will vary from person to person.

When it comes to helping people with their money and making financial decisions, I want my team, clients, vendors, and anyone I work with to know I'm having fun doing what I do. I want to create powerful ripples showing people they can work and enjoy life. I want what I do to draw people closer to their faith and strengthen their relationship with the Almighty. It drives me. It's what gets me out of bed each morning.

So how does one enjoy the fruit of their labor? I'm glad you asked.

Find Happiness in the Little Things

Caught in an endless, empty race without recognizing the prize, we run each day trying to fulfill our own expectations, other people's expectations, or simply blindly following rules we don't understand. Unfortunately, we forget one of the reasons for our existence: to enjoy it.

When is the last time you soaked at the moment or took time to breathe? True happiness is actually embracing the little joys in life. It could be watching the sunrise on a warm summer morning, drinking a cup of coffee, reading an amazing book, or watching your toddler sleep in peace. It comes from being grateful not only for when big things happen but for the small happiness you can find daily. For example, I have the same amount of joy when traveling across the world as when I watch my children play in the pool. I even enjoy spending time in the office and even waking up early to prepare for business meetings.

Do Something

Why not expand the joy in your life by regularly engaging in activities instead of binge-watching Netflix? Of course, there's nothing wrong with watching TV, but we weren't created to sit back and observe. We were created to do something! And who knows, by doing so, you could discover more talents that have been tucked away.

God doesn't want us to be discontented. We are supposed to be the kindest people on earth. So why not overflow with the joy of God? Jesus reassured his disciples and said, "These things I have spoken to you, that my *joy* may be in you, and that your *joy* may be full" (John 15:11, emphasis added) and "I am coming to you now, but I say these things while I am still in the world, so that they may have the *full measure of my joy* within them" (John 17:13, emphasis added).

God is not anti-fun. He wants us to have a rich, abundant life of enjoyment and fun. Don't you want the "full measure" of joy Jesus promised the disciples? I don't know about you, but I don't want to leave any room for chance. I want to receive everything God has for me—including joy.

Keep Learning

One of the best things you can do with money to maximize the happiness return on your financial investment is learning a new skill or hobby—creating an experience.

Take an art class or go skydiving. Get private golf or tennis lessons. Learn to dance salsa. Learning a new skill is fun and rewarding. It will broaden your horizons as a person, giving you new activities you can participate in for a lifetime of fulfillment while expanding your social circle simultaneously.

The thrill of exploration comes from expanding yourself. So travel to the place you've been on your bucket list and dreamed of; it's money well spent!

I'm learning that every single thing I do matters to God—from my productivity to how often I laugh. God designed us to have a heart that is full of life. Of course, I realize that fun can mean different things to different people, but what is something you haven't done in a long time that makes you say, in the words of the famous poet and philosopher Ice Cube, "Today was a good day!"

I believe that if God says He wants me to have life and have it to the fullest, that means He takes an interest in my work and the things that make me laugh and leave me free of worries. For me, that comes in the form of travel, spending time with friends and family, chopping it up over a glass of Uncle Nearest whiskey and a cigar. It comes from pulling pranks at the office, dancing, singing, and mocking epic moments as if I was a living, breathing TikTok video.

Joy isn't just found on our Instagram feeds or on the good days that have yet to come. So don't be deceived into thinking that having fun means less impact on the world. On the contrary, it equips us to have more impact. The world is still spinning, the work is still happening, and emails are still getting answered. But let's have some fun while we're at it.

Start Living

You have probably heard a tragic story about someone who pinched pennies to save for retirement, only to have their life cut short before enjoying the fruits of their labor. With all things in life, there is no promise that you will be able to enjoy life when you are older. So start living today—right now.

During the first five years of my insurance career, I spent time in nursing homes and retirement communities. I facilitated retirement planning and long-term care issues for self-paid and people on Medicaid who couldn't be cared for by their families. Some of them were there voluntarily, while others weren't. Those who were there because their family was busy tending to their own lives felt forced and were unhappy, and it showed. When I would do my workshops to provide them information, I would look at the attendees and see some with exasperation and others with enthusiasm. The ones who volunteered and paid to be there embraced it.

There was this one woman who stood out to me. She always attended my workshops. She was bright, glowed radiantly, and was 100 years old.

When class was over, I spoke with her. "You've obviously done well for yourself with your financial decisions. So why are you always sitting in my retirement planning workshop?" I asked.

Her body was frail, but her spirit and the focus of her eyes were infectious. She smiled, "Because I never let my education get in front of my learning."

Wow! I thought. "I really need to be learning from you," I responded.

After a bit more small talk, I left the nursing home with a different perspective. Here this woman was 100 years old, and she was still learning. She was still living. Her finances were set, and she was being taken care of, but her pursuit of learning and continuously improving stuck with me.

The opposite was true for some of the other people who were in attendance. It was as if they thought they had nothing to learn. They appeared to have nothing to look forward to, and the window to enjoy life had already happened—or didn't happen. Because of their perspective, they weren't happy with where they were.

It Takes Finances to Fund Your Fun

Having money in your bank account will not make you happy, but putting that money to good use can. Everywhere we look, we are inundated with the same message: "Buy, buy, buy your way to happiness!" While buying a new gadget or the first drive in a new car may be satisfying or thrilling, the thrill always fades, and we find ourselves back in the same place seeking the next purchase to keep the feeling going. Money doesn't buy happiness, but it can buy experiences. Start investing in experiences!

My kids have gone on some company trips with my wife and me. They spent time with influential people like former U.S. President George W. Bush and Eric Thomas (E.T.). We met Kobe Bryant, one of the greatest basketball players of all time.

They have heard Deion Sanders speak, amongst many other speakers making a global impact. We will value the memories we created with them for a lifetime.

I'm not just talking about this to name-drop. I'm sharing because I realize how those experiences impacted all of us. My kids have been around people they saw on T.V. or influencers on social media. They met people who followed their dreams.

My entire family can enjoy the fruit of my labor while also learning what it takes to have a work ethic. These will be the stories that my children tell my grandchildren, and their children tell their grandchildren. I have taken my children on trips to places I saw on a map or in magazines growing up. They have been and will be exposed to things I never was as a child, so I have no problem using finances to fund our fun—because the memories it creates are priceless.

God Gives the Desires of Your Heart

When you learn to read the Bible properly—and not merely as a collection of one-liners, weird stories, and sound bites—you'll find that some of the most famous passages take on different and deeper meanings.

We should begin with the most obvious fact. The phrase, "He will give you the desires of your heart," is only half of a verse, and we must consider the entire verse!

Psalm 37:4 says, "Delight yourself in the Lord, and he will give you the desires of your heart." But it's a conditional promise—if you delight yourself in the Lord, *then* He will give you the desires of your heart. In the immediate context, this is powerful. If we desire God, he will provide us with our desires, which must include him!

But there's more here. The first two verses of the psalm are an exhortation not to be envious of the wicked, "for they will soon fade like the grass." Then verses two to six exhibit a pattern, as the reader is urged to love the Lord in various ways, and he promises to respond and act. The parallel structure of these verses helps us understand what it means to "delight yourself in the Lord" and that God "will give you the desires of your heart."

Those that profess that they have and follow their faith should trust in their Creator and do good, commit [their] way to the Lord. Then God will grant them to dwell in the land and befriend faithfulness, he will act, and he will bring forth [their] righteousness as the light.

Notice the circular pattern here—the more we commit our ways to God and trust in Him, the more we will have faith in Him—and we receive our heart's desires. Matthew 6:33 says it best, "But seek first his kingdom and his righteousness, and all these things will be given to you as well."

In the book of Ecclesiastes, Solomon observed that nothing is better for us than to rejoice and do good in our lives. He also says that it is God's gift for every man and woman to eat, drink and enjoy the good of all their labor. According to this, God wants us to enjoy our lives.

If you do not honor and obey the Lord, it is possible other people will enjoy the fruit of your labor—people you don't even know or like. They will take your land and the fruit of your hard work. You will be indebted to them because "the rich rule over the poor and the borrower is servant to the lender" (Proverbs 22:7).

We are all given the same amount of time and choose what to do with it. If you fail to maximize each day, it's your loss, and you can't get it back. The time you have is the time you have. You get to decide how you spend the time, just as you choose how you spend your money. It is never the case of us not having enough time to do things, but the issue of whether we want to do them and where they fall in our priorities.

God's promises never change. He is committed to providing fulfillment to those who apply His word to their lives. I believe the only way to have a fulfilling life is to enjoy and stop trying to escape it.

Design a Life You Don't Want to Escape

For most people, travel, and vacation is a means of escape. It's natural to want a break from routine, work, and responsibilities. That makes sense for how people at the office spend their two weeks of paid time off each year. They want to feel refreshed and renewed after sitting on a beach in Cabo to distract them from work emails.

It appears they are just running away from underlying problems they don't want to address. Most people know the travel-as-escape feeling in terms of fight-or-flight: how we naturally (and physically) react when faced with conflict or situations we choose to ignore.

I started questioning why someone would need to escape from their life. I didn't want to live like this. I started looking at people who always went away for Christmas and spring breaks—realizing it was an effort to distract themselves from their current life. I don't knock anyone traveling during those times, but I realized I didn't want to be a person who had a life they wanted to just really avoid.

I had to rethink what the word vacation meant, so I began studying the word's origin and etymology. It comes from a combination of two words. The Latin root word "vacō": to be empty; vacate: to vacate an area is to go away from it, emptying yourself from it; vacuity: the total absence of matter; and "tion": a suffix occurring in words of Latin origin, meaning a state of being. So vacation meant to remove oneself from a current state of being.[16]

I began asking myself if I wanted to remove myself from my life. Then I began reframing how I saw traveling and life. I started to see trips as 'tax-deductible business trips'— a mix of entrepreneurship, business purposes, and entertainment. We sandwich a bit of fun while still accomplishing things to grow our economic endeavors. It was a time to reset and regroup instead of running from responsibilities.

---

[16]https://unabridged.merriam-webster.com/

When most people take time off, they dread returning to work. So on their last day of vacation, most people would be saying to themselves, "I don't want to go back to work! It ended so soon!" This is where many timeshare salespeople get you emotionally to buy a "lifetime of vacations because your family deserves it."

I came to the realization that I did not want to feel the uneasiness of returning to the office when a trip came to an end. For this reason, we've restructured our perspective and ways of "taking a vacation" and instead called them "tax-deductible business trips" filled with purpose, fun, and time to recharge and energize. By the time we reach the last day, we cannot wait to return home and crush it with the new ideas or strategies we want to incorporate.

I am constantly fueled and excited when I leave a trip to come back home. I can't wait to put into play the ideas I came up with while I was away. I genuinely enjoy the fruit of my labor, no matter where I am or what I do. I'd love for you to say the same!

12

Create a Purpose-Filled Life

"Behind me is infinite power. Before me is endless possibility, around me is boundless opportunity. My strength is mental,- physical and spiritual."

– 50 Cent

The purpose of life is not supposed to be: to work, pay bills, retire and die. In our pursuit of wealth, success, and prosperity, finding and following our purpose in alignment with what our creator wants for us is the ultimate source of fulfillment. We have to be clear about what we want and trust that our lives are in his hands to live a purpose-filled life.

When our hearts are aligned with God's purpose for us, we are not only satisfied but man, are we happy. When I look at people in pursuit of their desires, I see them in constant recreation, always in pursuit of the next best version of themselves.

Created to Create

Genesis 1:27 says, "So God created man in His own image; in the image of God He created him; male and female he created them."

The very first introduction to the nature of God, as revealed through Scripture, is that God is creative. The Bible doesn't open with accounts of God's grace, love, power, holiness, or any of the most common characteristics we know and love about our heavenly Father. Instead, the Bible opens with the story of how God created something from nothing. Then, in the same chapter, Scripture describes how God creates man in His own image.

When God created the heavens and the earth, Scripture indicates that the earth was without form and void. Essentially, God brought organization and order to emptiness and chaos. He created something out of nothing. The Lord's *enterprise and business* is the world He created, in which we and all humanity live. Based on God's creation of the entire universe, I'd say God qualifies as the first entrepreneur.

We share our Creator's creative abilities and attributes as people created in God's image. Simply put, we are also made to create. God imparted the ability to create, build, dream, invent, organize and lead, among many other valuable skills. Creating something from nothing is the very embodiment of what it means to be an entrepreneur. Entrepreneurs build things that haven't existed before. That's what God did when He created you, me, and the rest of creation.

Every little thing we start is a creation, a miracle by itself. Think for a second: before we activate the universe to make things happen, it's not in existence. This book started from mere thoughts that were transferred to notes on paper. Those same notes turned into sentences. The end result is what you are holding in your hands.

Picture a cup of coffee in your mind. Before you pour the water, add the brown powder and put some heat on it, there is nothing there. Separate pieces of matter, drifting around in your environment without any intention to glue them together. It was you who changed this and manifested a cup of coffee where there was nothing before.

As kids, we used our imaginations. Our brains were our canvasses, and we inherently understood that we could use our minds to create absolutely anything and spend the day living it out. So we were in a constant state of dreams and creativity.

Over the course of a few decades, the world tends to have a way of stifling your creativity. If you want to enjoy life, you have to make time to do what you loved to do when you were young. Working today has provided us with the ability to spur creation and innovation.

If you don't have a job you love, build something you love! We have the creative nature of God dwelling within us. We should be the ones creating and building the greatest companies in the world. Having God as our business partner is the greatest competitive advantage an entrepreneur or business person could possibly ask for!

Follow Your Dreams

Steve Jobs once said, "For the past thirty-three years, I have looked in the mirror every morning and asked myself: If today were the last day of my life, would I want to do what I am about to do today? And whenever the answer has been no for too many days in a row, I know I need to change something."

There is a scene from the movie *Up in the Air* where George Clooney's character terminates a man in his mid-fifties. Decades before, he had accepted a job and subsequently gave up on his dream of becoming a chef.

Fast-forward to the meeting in the office, add a mortgage payment, wife, a kid with chronic illness, and a bad case of life sucks.

Ryan Bingham, played by George Clooney, asked the man, "How much did they pay you to give up on your dreams?"

He responded, "I'm making $95k now, but I started at $27k."

After telling him that getting fired was a wake-up call, he asked, "Why do people love pro-athletes?"

For those who have seen the movie, you know the first response. It was about having sex with lingerie models. But after further clarification, he specified, "Why do *kids* love athletes?"

After a brief pause, he said, "Because they don't give up on their dreams."

My question to you is, are you following your dreams? Are your kids following athletes, or are they following you? Of course, parents want their kids to do their best, but are you giving it your all? Are you giving life your all? Are you having fun doing it?

If you aren't, you can easily get into a place of playing the blame game because you aren't happy. You can't even get upset at your kid for not striving for more or doing well in school or sports. Kids will follow what you show them, not what you tell them. Living a life of clocking in and out without a moment of happiness will weigh on you.

It is possible to have a career or business that you love. As you're reading this, I hope you have something that brings you happiness. If you don't, you might need to ask yourself what Steve Jobs asked himself and consider doing something different. Think about a world without Apple, MacBooks, iPads, iPhones, and AirDrop. Crazy right? What is the world missing from you not being in a position of greater creativity, passion, and contribution? Don't go another day without working toward your dreams.

FOUR STAGES OF INCOME

I know I had an entire section on finances, but I wanted to share people's four stages of income while working toward their purpose.

Survivability: This stage is about survival. You are fighting to stay above water and, more than likely, living paycheck to paycheck. Unfortunately, the sad reality is that 48% of all people live this way. Even worse, those earning $100k are also finding themselves in that bind.

I remember doing a workshop in San Jose, California, a few years ago. I picked up a newspaper in the hotel. It says the low income was $117,00 for nine counties in the Bay Area.

Up from 29%, over 38% of those earning six figures live paycheck to paycheck too. A recent Bloomberg report stated that one-third of those making a $250k salary is beginning to live paycheck to paycheck.[17]

Status: This stage is about promotion. Let's say you start a career in sales. You close some deals and find yourself making more money. This stage helps you embrace more risks of the unknown.

You reward yourself with a new home, car, jewelry, vacations, and clothes.

Common, everyday expenses are no longer a concern, and you don't think twice about swiping the credit card as much as you used to, worrying if it will decline.

Freedom: This is the stage when you've finally started saving, investing, and reinvesting. Your small practice has grown into

[17]Tanzi, Alexander, One-Third of Americans Making $250,000 Live Paycheck-to-Paycheck, Survey Finds, June 2021

a scalable business. Your corporate gig has got you on more frequent bonuses, company cars, jets, and lodging usage.

For once, you have a massive leftover balance of cash coming into the next month. You finally have more money than month leftover instead of the other way around.

Your income exceeds your expenses. As a result, you have more assets and net worth than debt on the balance sheet to worry about.

In addition, many emergencies that popped up previously to derail and frustrate you are now immediately solved with the stroke of a check or swipe of a credit card.

You now have the opportunity to retire your parents, take on the burden of the bills from a relative and absorb them into your family payroll without batting an eye.

Purpose: This is the stage when you realize that money is an amazing tool. There are only so many steak dinners, exotic cars, homes, and a once-in-a-lifetime vacations you can take. Now, you get quickly bored with these moments and seek a deeper meaning to it all.

You begin every thought and direction of your finances to ensure that it makes a difference in the world. There is a meaning behind your efforts and effective use of the money you dole out.

You seek to make sure everyone that comes across you, directly or indirectly, that is the radius of your brand leaves better than when they first found you. All in all, to achieve this gradual ascent into the different phases of income, you make it about others.

This cannot be done if you operate from a scarcity mentality. Instead, you limit yourself with the unconscious thought that there is a limited amount of resources, opportunities, personnel, and relationships.

However, if you feel there is a vast amount of abundance where *everyone* can earn and enjoy what they work towards, you'll find it rewarding to lift and celebrate someone else winning even though you are not at this particular time.

You just know if you out improve, out strategize, outwork, and outlast yourself, you'll soon discover the next best version of yourself.

Winning in business and your finances doesn't mean that there is a win-lose situation. That the only way you win is because you had taken away from someone and they lost in a confrontation with you.

The best way to win is to find win-win scenarios which galvanize relationships for the long term and fulfillment in helping others succeed. This, in turn, becomes deeply authentic and genuine in your daily efforts to grow the potential of anything you lay your hands on.

PURSUE PRODUCTIVITY

I don't look at the calendar as regular weekdays. Instead, I call them Focus, Buffer, or Recreation Days. I look at my day as three days in one. Morning is one day, Afternoon the next, and Evening the third. I'm either on, off, or recreating myself, but I know being productive is more than checking things off the box.

It's about structuring my life to create and execute—whether it's content creation, recruiting new candidates or developing new ones, expansion opportunities, or just for fun, I designed a schedule that was suitable for me.

My days are highlighted in colors so I can see which days I need to add, reduce or delegate.

Green: Focus Day: WORKING IN THE BUSINESS

These days are money-making activities.

I'm closing deals, sitting down with clients, interviewing potential candidates in a recruiting interview, and creating strategic alliances. Not to mention, I interview vendors and partners and bridge businesses together and use every meeting to develop and drive revenue or produce content.

Red: Buffer/Preparation Day: WORKING ON THE BUSINESS

These are the days we have team meetings, company events, conventions, retreats, leadership development, and reviewing financial statements.

I am putting notes together for a proposal/team meeting, and recording a new episode for YouTube, creating a series, or developing new projects.

Blue: Recreation Day: RECREATING MYSELF

These are the calm, peaceful, tranquil days I use to focus on myself and my family. I do not work on or in the business.

I can get more done by compartmentalizing my activities; therefore, I do not stress out about things overlapping. This is important to do, or you burn out. Entrepreneurs or anyone who works remotely, if you don't have a structured schedule, it can interfere with creativity. Just like you need to incorporate a schedule, you must prioritize rest. You can recharge your emotions through quietness, solitude, or recreation, which can rejuvenate you.

Live with No Regrets

In the series Friday Nights Lights, before every game, the team declares, "Clear eyes, full heart, can't lose," before they take to the field. It's like a recipe for a good life. If you approach each moment, milestone, and interaction with clear eyes, intention, purpose, and an open mind and heart, you can't lose.

Looking back on my time in the Marine Corps, I am still connected to several Marines who were battle buddies with me through different deployments. Over the years, we had several conversations. I have asked them if they were finally following what they wanted to do or just settling for a job. Instead of answering the question, they put it back on me and told me I was smarter than them. But I wasn't. I haven't ever been smarter than them. They were just as capable as I was. I just wanted something different and wouldn't settle.

It reminded me of when I was at the retirement home looking at the group of people with pained expressions trying to fade into the background during my workshops. Some of the ones who attended seemed to be living in regret. Whether it was people they should have reconciled with or jobs they never pursued, they accepted things as they were and never had closure.

Instead of asking, "What will I do in retirement?" ask, "What will I regret?" It's a simple way to become more in the present and ensure you're living for now versus later. My fellow Marines still have time, but they have to decide what they will do in the next twenty to thirty years.

There are no guarantees in life. Whether it's losing a loved one, having a physical ailment, or other challenges, plans can quickly change and put long-held desires and dreams out of reach for good. While people believe they will have additional time and freedom to focus on important areas of life, there are several things you can do now to make the most of your current time.

Let Go of the Past

I'm often asked how I overcame PTSD. I am not a medical expert, but I experienced depression because I was still living in the past. I was stuck in the past from things that happened in the military and growing up.

I did not want to remain despondent, so I went to counseling and began working through what was troubling me. I was given a certificate after completing the program. I wish I had kept it. I would have framed it as a reminder that I didn't have to live in the past. But, instead, I shredded it to symbolize that I would never go back to that precarious place again.

Letting go means you have to move forward. If I were driving a car and continued to look in the rearview mirror, I would lose sight of what was in front of me. I would possibly wreck and hurt myself or, worse, someone else. Looking out of the windshield is so much better. It's bigger, broader, and in the direction I want to go. When I stopped looking behind me, the past started getting smaller, and I got happier.

If you've never seen the movie *Saving Private Ryan*, I don't want to ruin it for you, but there's a part that impacts me significantly. The men in *Saving Private Ryan* were sent to find and bring home Pvt. James Ryan, a paratrooper who dropped somewhere into Normandy on June 6, 1944. Unbeknownst to him, Ryan's three brothers were killed in separate operations. So to spare his mother more anguish, it was mandated Ryan be found and brought home at all costs.

Fast forward to the ending of the movie when Pvt. Ryan is at the cemetery with his wife. Ryan stood beside his friend's grave and talked to him briefly. He then asked his wife if he was a good man and lived a good life; which she confirmed; allowing him to feel he made their sacrifice worthwhile. He saluted the grave as the American flag was blowing in the background, with his family standing around him in admiration.

It's easy to focus on how much work we have to do and how far away our big goal is, but it's equally important to celebrate how far we've come. Taking time to celebrate our progress, even if we are celebrating baby steps, keeps us feeling accomplished and not overwhelmed.

Don't try to change everything all at once. You'll feel much more accomplished and more likely to set and reach other goals, including how to create a purpose-filled life.

Finding a path for my life, led through faith and God shining a light during the whole journey, keeps me fulfilled. It helps me serve in many ways as I focus on what I can do today. I feel I am living a purpose-filled life helping myself first so I can serve others and do what God has destined for me. You can do the same. There is nothing special, gifted, or extraordinary about me. If I can figure it out, so can you.

God plants dreams in us just like He gives us specific talents and gifts. If you have a dream that just won't go away, and that dream will somehow make the world a better place, start planning to achieve it. Write out exactly what your vision is, get up, and go after it!

Conclusion

Thank you for investing the time to read up to this point. By taking this step, you've shown you want to keep improving your life. In the industry I'm in, I interact with a lot of people. So one thought that always comes to mind is how can I make this person better after meeting with me than before they met me.

Let these final pages serve as a time of reflection. Seeing who you are aids in having a better understanding of who you want to become and what you want out of life. It's a difficult but necessary assessment.

A life built on a solid foundation of values and principles can remove limitations. Allow room for failure and grace instead of punishing yourself for never meeting perceived expectations. These things play a role in your mindset, which spills over into how you live.

Before it's time to put the things you've learned to practice, understand that you must be consistent and persevere because how you started isn't necessarily how you finish. It reminds me of one of the best players who was almost overlooked.

During his final days of college, Tom Brady's coach received only one call of interest from the NFL for his star quarterback. But that didn't deter Brady and his goal of playing football in the NFL. Instead, he set his sights on the NFL draft and had high hopes of getting picked up early. However, Brady would face disappointment once again. Instead of getting chosen early, it wasn't until the 6th round as the 199th pick that he would eventually get to breathe a sigh of relief.

Tom Brady was underrated and underestimated. In fact, his draft report from the 2000 NFL draft noted the following qualities:[18]

- Poor Build | Skinny
- Lacks Great Physical Stature and Strength
- Lacks Mobility and Ability to Avoid The Rush
- Lacks a Really Strong Arm
- Can't Drive The Ball Down Field
- Doesn't Throw a Really Tight Spiral
- System-Type Player Who Can Get Exposed if Forced to Adlib
- Gets Knocked Down Easily

---

[18]www.skysports.com

Ouch! That was a bit discouraging. There is no doubt that Brady wasn't the highest rated, he wasn't the best athlete, and he didn't have the best numbers or mechanics, but he did have the qualities that have proven to matter most: heart and determination.

No measurable drill or ruler can see or measure the size of a champion's heart. No one knew Tom Brady's thoughts or willingness to commit to deepening the faith that he had in himself and what he could accomplish.

During his second year with the New England Patriots, after starting QB Drew Bledsoe was sidelined due to an injury, Brady took to the field; he prepared for the opportunity while no one was looking or paying attention. And for the past twenty-plus years, Brady has been stacking and collecting achievements, accolades, and championships like a kid collecting comic books.

For the past twenty years, Tom Brady has proven to himself and the world that he is the best of the best in football. He may arguably be one of the most outstanding athletes, in any sport, of all time. He has the evidence, stats, and facts to prove it. Tom Brady didn't have all the sought-after qualities and attributes that the other quarterbacks had, but he had the qualities that mattered most. And the same applies to you.

Maybe you have been overlooked or experienced a reversal of fortune, but what are you doing about it? The main driver behind Brady's greatness and the success ethos that has guided him to become the living legend is something we've all come to admire. There is power in repetition, which is the mother of learning and the architect of accomplishment.

Make sure to remember that life is not one short race; it's a marathon of marathons. If you believe you can succeed in life, in spite of any circumstances that may appear to be headed in the direction of failure, you will win these marathons.

I have to stay focused on the reason why I do what I do. I will make my family name known, be respected, and create wealth for generations to come. What is the purpose that drives your actions? Why do you workout? Why do you eat healthily? Why do you have the goals you have? Why do you want the things you desire? What is your plan to get there? I want you to keep these questions at the forefront of your mind as this book comes to an end.

When times of trial come, faith can give you the strength to press forward and face hardships with courage—and when you don't feel it, you can open this book again. I encourage you to borrow the courage in this book and the courage of others who have gone before you if you feel you are at a standstill or just stuck.

If you believe in yourself, take responsibility, and take ownership of your life, actions, results, and responses, you will be fueled with the perseverance to reach your goals. You will make excuses or even self-sabotage if you don't believe in yourself. Believe in the power you have when you set your mind to something. Set your sights on something with determination, diligence, and the firm resolve to remain on that path! Tell yourself you can do the necessary work, align with a proven mentor, and associate with like-minded people, and you will succeed.

It is a daily choice whether or not to remain hindered by the pains, disappointments, and failures of the past or use faith to trust where you need to be strengthened and developed—especially when it comes to mindset, morals, and money. Living by core values sounds easy—at least in theory, but that's not always the case. Yet, it helps us develop the characteristics and behaviors that motivate us and guide our decisions—in good or bad times.

Too often, we try to talk ourselves out of taking risks. We might not give our best effort because doing so might attract more attention if we were to fail. Often we don't want people to know we failed, so we say we tried. But as the great philosopher, Yoda said, "Do or do not; there is no try." So go out and give 100% of your effort behind every new idea or strategy you decide to implement.

You'll inevitably collect a few failures that you can proudly hang on your wall as reminders, but in the process, you will also collect a number of successes. You have access to opportunities; you have to pay attention. Some doors are going to open. You have to walk through them.

Success is measured by faith and obedience. Never in a million years did I think I would be in sales. Never in a million years did I think I would be an entrepreneur. Never in a million years would I think I would be selling life insurance. Never in a million years would I think I'd be a millionaire in business with bigger thinkers, creators, and implementers. But here I am today.

I want to set an example for others and teach as many people as I can what I have learned. I've magnified my dreams, and those who invoke the same ethos can magnify their dreams too. You have the power to do so much more. If you think like a millionaire and strategize with faith, you can become a faith-made millionaire.

Acknowledgements

Many mentors, partners, colleagues, staff, friends, and family have contributed over the years to developing the principles I live by. I appreciate each and every one who has crossed my path.

Patrick Bet-David, it has been an honor to have worked by your side to witness a visionary's declarations to make history come true. You're a once-in-a-generation leader, mentor, and icon. I am grateful to call you a friend. The world is a profoundly better place because of the Bet-David name.

In addition to my mentor, I want to recognize the significance of the co-founders of PHP Agency. Jorge Pelayo, Jose and Marlene Gaytan, Jon Mason, Rodolfo and Cecy Vargas, you have used the gifts and talents God has given you. As a result, millions of families have been impacted by your courage to start a company that faced so much opposition. One of those families is mine. You have shown the world what following your faith can do to transform lives, starting with you own.

I appreciate and want to thank the leadership team of the MoneySmartMovement: Jon Mason, Chris and Vicena Hart, Kehinde and Eli Thomas, Edward and Jamie Musgrove, Ellis and Jasmine Suazo, Bill and Kim Korman, Reuben and Sable Otey, Vic and Ana Landor, Chris and Evelyn Richardson, Pastor Rashawn and Wanda Bey. Thank you for tirelessly laboring with me; it's an honor to be in business with you. Let's continue to march forward toward our vision to transform the thoughts, behaviors, and actions that create wealth. The history books will write about you being the *best* ever to do this.

Prayer of Salvation

I didn't think I ever needed a Savior until life kept hitting me over and over, strinking me down fflat on my face. I kept trying it "my way," thinking that just trying to be a good person was good enough.

It wasn't until my thirtieth birthday, when I woke up driving intoxicated on the other side of the street, almost hitting a car driving the opposite way, that I decided my life needed to change. I could have killed myself. Worse, I could have killed someone's loved one and orphaned my kids, whom I was raising as a single father. I don't know your present situation, but if you're still reading this, maybe you're going through a difficult time and looking for answers. No judgment, just love.

If you're looking to connect the dots here on Earth with your faith and your Creator in heaven but don't know what to call him, consider the name of Jesus.

He said, "Come to me, all you who are weary and burdened, and I will give you rest. Take my yoke upon you and learn from me, for I am gentle and humble in heart, and you will find rest for your souls for my yoke is easy and my burden is light" (Matthew 11:28-30).

Peace, direction, and having someone to place my faith in brought me clarity. If you feel this solution could be for you, say the name "Jesus" and pray this prayer:

Lord Jesus,

I bring my worst to you and ask for your forgiveness. Please come into my heart as my Lord and Savior. Take complete control of my life and help me walk in Your footsteps daily by the power of the Holy Spirit. Thank you, Lord, for saving me and answering my prayer.

Amen.

The heavens just rejoiced when you prayed that prayer, accepting Jesus Christ into your life. Know that you have a fellow brother in me and many brothers and sisters in Christ throughout the world. Find a local church you can regularly attend to deepen your faith and your walk with Christ.

If you'd like, please send me an IG story and tag me @ MoneySmartGuy with #FaithMadeMillionaire telling me you've prayed this prayer. I'd love to share in your newfound joy and peace.

God bless you.

CONNECT WITH MATT SAPAULA FOR:

1. Future appearances, events, workshops, masterminds, and online meetings
2. Implementing financial strategies contained in this book
3. Refer you to a local professional trained with this mindset, morals, and financial strategies in our national network
4. Training and mentoring as an insurance agency builder working alongside our team
5. An interview for your TV segment, radio show, or podcast
6. Booking as a speaker for your event or conference
7. Mutually beneficial strategic partnerships if you are a realtor, mortgage loan officer or income tax, professional

Please submit your information if you would like to be contacted at www.MoneySmartGuy.com or call 469.828.8800.

Follow Matt Sapaula on social media:

YouTube - 7 Figure Squad

Instagram @MoneySmartGuy

Twitter @MoneySmartGuy

Facebook @MoneySmartGuy - Matt Sapaula

TikTok @MoneySmartGuy

Resources

The Power of Positive Thinking by Dr. Norman Vincent Peale

The Magic of Thinking Big by David J. Schwartz

Secrets of the Millionaire Mind by T. Harv Eker

Wealth for All: Living a Life of Success at the Edge of Your Ability by Idowu Koyenikan

Money, Possessions and Eternity by Randy Alcorn

Rich Dad, Poor Dad by Robert Kiyosaki

Why the Rich Get Richer by Robert Kiyosaki

8 Lessons in Military Leadership by Robert Kiyosaki

Missed Fortune 101 by Douglas R. Andrew

How I Raised Myself from Failure to Success in Selling by Frank Bettge

The Power of Positive Thinking by Peale, Dr. Norman Vincent

The Magic of Thinking Big by David J. Schwartz

21 Irrefutable Laws of Leadership by John C. Maxwell

Leadership Bible by John C. Maxwell

25 Laws of Doing the Impossible by Patrick Bet-David

Life of an Entrepreneur in 90 Days by Patrick Bet-David

God Wants You to be Rich by Paul Zane Pilzer

Secrets of the Millionaire Mind by T. Harv Eker

Extreme Ownership: How U.S. Navy SEALs Lead and Win by Jocko Willink

Relentless by Tim Grover

Richest Man Who Ever Lived by Steven K. Scott

The Millionaire Fast Lane by M. J. DeMarco

Your Next Five Moves by Patrick Bet-David

Sources

Introduction

1. Megan Brenan and Nicole Willcoxon. Record-High 50% of Americans Rate U.S. Moral Values as 'Poor'.

https://news.gallup.com/poll/393659/record-high-americans-rate-moral-values-poor.aspx

Chapter 1

2. The phrase is often attributed to war correspondent Ernie Pyle as an aphorism used to argue that people will believe in, or hope for, a higher power in times of fear or stress, such as during war ("in foxholes"). In our case, it was salvation through Jesus Christ.

https://www.merriam-webster.com/dictionary/foxhole

Chapter 4

3. Peter Churchouse, Stansberry Churchouse Research Dec 17, 2017,How one of the richest dynasties in American history lost its fortune

Chapter 5

4. Paul Rudder How much money does Michael Jordan earn? Salary, net worth and endorsements, February 2022

https://en.as.com/en/2022/02/20/nba/1645333569_647331.html

Chapter 6

Mensa Otabil, *Beyond the Rivers of Ethiopia: A Biblical Revelation on God's Purpose for the Black Race* (Accra: Altar Media, 2004), 8, 64.

Matthew Ashimolowo, The Coming Wealth Transfer (London: Mattyson Media, 2006), 193–94.

Chapter 7

5. CPI for all items rises 1.3% in June; gasoline, shelter, food indexes rise, June 2022

https://www.bls.gov/cpi/

Chapter 8

6. BBC News, Millions become millionaires during Covid pandemic, June 2021

https://www.bbc.com/news/business-57575077

7. Investopedia, The Number of Millionaires Continues to Increase, Charlotte Wold, Updated January 2022

https://www.investopedia.com/news/number-millionaires-continues-increase/

8. Jenny McCall, Number of global millionaires to grow significantly, June 2021

https://capital.com/number-of-global-millionaires-to-grow

9. By Lindsay Dunsmuir, Explainer: Federal Reserve's taper: How does it work?, November 2021

https://www.reuters.com/business/federal-reserves-taper-how-does-it-work-2021-11-03/

10.Daniel Levi, 80% of all US dollars in existence were printed in the last 22 months (from $4 trillion in January 2020 to $20 trillion in October 2021)

https://techstartups.com/2021/12/18/80-us-dollars-existence-printed-january-2020-october-2021/

11. Ben Casselman, Highest Record of U.S. Workers Quitting, November 2021

https://www.nytimes.com/2021/11/12/business/economy/jobs-labor-openings-quit.html

12. Jessica Dickler, CNBC, Life Changes, Americans Living Paycheck to Paycheck, March 2022https://www.cnbc.com/2022/03/08/as-prices-rise-64-percent-of-americans-live-paycheck-to-paycheck.html

Chapter 9

13. Rubin G. Better Than Before: Mastering the Habits of Our Everyday Lives. Toronto, Ontario: Penguin Random House, Doubleday Canada; 2015.

14. University of Wisconsin - Madison National Library of Medicine

https://www.ncbi.nlm.nih.gov/pmc/articles/PMC3374921 increased%20risk%20of%20premature%20death

Chapter 10

15. Julia Oates, Just Disciple,Types of Fasting & Whats Right for You

https://justdisciple.com/fasting-types/

Chapter 11

16.www.merriam-webster.com/words-at-play/vacation-definition-history

Chapter 12

17. Tanzi, Alexander, One-Third of Americans Making $250,000 Live Paycheck-to-Paycheck, Survey Finds, June 2021

https://www.bloomberg.com/news/articles/2022-06-01/a-third-of-americans-making-250-000-say-costs-eat-entire-salary

Conclusion

18. Sky Sports, Davie Currie, Tom Brady: Goodbye to the GOAT, February 2021

https://www.skysports.com/nfl/story-telling/12118/12531669/tom-brady-goodbye-to-the-goat-as-seven-time-super-bowl-winner-retires